# After This

Also by Claire Bidwell Smith

*Conscious Grieving: A Transformative Approach to Healing from Loss*

*Anxious Grief: A Clinician's Guide to Supporting Grieving Clients Experiencing Anxiety, Panic, and Fear*

*Anxiety: The Missing Stage of Grief*

*The Rules of Inheritance*

"Soothing and informative..."
—The New York Times

# After This

## WHEN LIFE IS OVER, WHERE DO WE GO?

CLAIRE BIDWELL SMITH

Copyright © 2015 by Claire Bidwell Smith

All rights reserved

ISBN 9798878693264

10  9  8  7  6  5  4  3  2  1

Set in Goudy Oldstyle Std
Designed by Eve Kirch

Cover Design by Lindsey Strickland

AUTHOR'S NOTE
This is a work of nonfiction. Some names and identifying details have been altered in order to protect the privacy of particular individuals. Everything herein is based on the author's own memories and recollections.

PUBLISHER'S NOTE
While the author has made every effort to provide accurate telephone numbers, Internet addresses, and other contact information at the time of publication, neither the publisher nor the author assumes any responsibility for errors or for changes that occur after publication. Further, publisher does not have any control over and does not assume any responsibility for author or third-party websites or their content.

To Julie Sherali and Abigail Freeman—our friendships made me a better person, and for that I will be forever grateful.

To my daughters, Veronica and Juliette—I am honored to be your mother. I love you to the moon and back.

# PREFACE

For my daughters' second and fifth birthdays, which fall just a week apart, I gift them a butterfly kit. A week later we receive a small jar of live caterpillars in the mail and watch with fascination as they crawl around their tiny plastic habitat, eventually making their way to the top, where they spin themselves into little ethereal cocoons.

My youngest, Juliette, is entranced by the caterpillars. She has a natural affinity for any kind of living creature, constantly distracted by the sight of a dog walking down the sidewalk, or even a roly poly crossing our path as we make our way to the garage before school.

Every morning we check on the cocoons. Three of the four caterpillars have spun a chrysalis, but the fourth hangs from the side of the jar, looking a little thinner and drier each day. I don't think that one's going to make it.

Finally, following the directions, I carefully transfer the cocoons to a netted habitat that came with the kit. We peer at them each day, waiting with anticipation to see them emerge as butterflies. The fourth caterpillar has made it to the top of the jar, but has not formed a cocoon and has now turned black and stiff.

# Preface

One morning after I drop the girls at school, I return to the house to find that one of the butterflies has emerged. It perches gently outside its now-empty cocoon, on the side of the net. A splash of what looks like blood is smeared on the paper to which the cocoon is attached, and I read that this is normal and that it is called meconium, a by-product that the butterfly did not need as it made its physical transformation.

When I pick up the girls that afternoon I excitedly tell them that one of the butterflies has arrived. We stop at my friend Joan's house to gather some flowers from her garden, as the kit suggests placing some at the bottom of the net, along with some sugar water for the butterflies to feast on.

When we arrive home the other two butterflies have also emerged, and enthralled we watch them, all of us seated around the dining room table. They are beautiful and delicate, their wings opening and closing, their antennae swiveling about as they take in the world.

"Mom," my oldest, whom I have nicknamed Vera, asks, "how did they become butterflies?"

I read a bit to her from the guide that was included with the kit, about the actual physiology of how caterpillars become butterflies, but the explanation seems stiff and scientific compared to the miraculous transformation we are witnessing in front of us. It seems nearly impossible that these elegant insects with their patterned wings were once fuzzy little caterpillars.

For two days we observe the butterflies, feeding them flowers and fruit and sugar water. I explain to the girls that we cannot keep them, and that the next morning we will take them out in the backyard and release them.

"They deserve to live in the world," I tell the girls. They nod at me solemnly, agreeing.

# Preface

The next morning when we wake up, only two of the butterflies are perched on the side of the net. I find the third one immobile at the bottom of the enclosure, obviously dead. I feel a great wave of remorse that this butterfly did not make it to our release day, never getting to experience what it would be like to fly into the sky.

"One of the butterflies died," I tell the girls, unable to hide the note of sadness from my voice.

"Oh, no," Vera exclaims. "What do we do with it?"

"Well, I think we should first release the other two, and then we'll bury this one and have a little ceremony for it," I tell her.

The girls nod at me with serious looks on their little faces, and I'm struck by how easily they absorb the ideas I offer them.

Outside in the backyard we open up the netted habitat and watch as the two live butterflies soar up into the bright blue California sky. We watch them until we can't see them anymore, and Jules dances about excitedly.

"Flying, Mama!" she says, over and over again. "They're flying!"

"They are, sweetie," I say, smiling.

Finally, I remove the third butterfly from the bottom of the enclosure and I let the girls hold it gently in their palms, all of us marveling over its intricate beauty.

"Where should we put it, Mama?" Vera asks.

"I think we should bury it over there," I say, pointing to a bush full of flowering white roses in the corner of the yard.

Together the three of us walk over to the bush and kneel down in the dirt. Jules holds the butterfly carefully while Vera digs a shallow grave with one of my salad serving spoons. Gently we place the butterfly in the soil and then we cover it with fallen rose petals that we have collected.

"Let's all say a few words of thanks to the butterfly," I say, and we take hands, closing our eyes.

# Preface

"Thank you for allowing us to be part of your life, butterfly," I say. "I'm sorry that you didn't get to fly into the world, but we are so grateful that we got to see you transform from a caterpillar."

"Thank you, butterfly," Vera says. "You were very pretty."

"Thanks, buttafly," Jules says quietly.

Inside, the house feels a little emptier.

"Buttafly died," Jules murmurs, over and over again.

I squat down in front of both girls, tugging at their hands, knowing that they are already shifting direction and ready to disappear into their room to play.

"The butterfly did die," I say to them. "But remember how the butterfly was first a caterpillar?"

They nod at me.

"And then it went into its cocoon?"

They nod again.

"Well, now it's in the ground, which is like another cocoon, and it's going to go through another transformation. It will emerge into something else eventually," I explain.

"Like into another butterfly?" Vera asks excitedly.

"Not exactly. But it will become part of the earth again, and its energy will go on to be something else. Maybe a flower in the rosebush, or maybe something we can't even imagine."

"Is that what happens when *we* die?" Vera asks.

"I think it is," I say. "And either way, the love we have for the butterfly doesn't change. Just like when a person dies, that love we feel for them doesn't disappear. And neither does theirs for us."

"I still love the butterfly," Vera says, mirroring my statement.

"Love the buttafly," Jules mimics.

"Yes, we all love the butterfly. The one in the ground, and the ones that flew up into the sky. That's what's important."

# Preface

I release my daughters' hands and they scamper off to play. I stand up and watch them from the doorway for a moment, thinking about how the only thing I really want them to understand about death is that it does not change love.

---

In her later years, after she had done extensive research on the afterlife, Elisabeth Kübler-Ross came to the conclusion that "death is but a transition from this life to another existence." I believe this to be true as well.

Like Kübler-Ross, I've been thinking about death for a long time. First as a result of the personal losses I've experienced, and now as a result of the work I do helping people navigate their own grief processes. What happens when we die? I've been asking myself this question for most of my life.

Thinking about what happens when someone dies is a natural part of the grief process. But not only that; it is part of the *life* process. How we make sense of our time here has an enormous impact on how we live our lives, how we develop relationships, and how we plan for the future. Death is a part of life, but one that we're not always so good at looking at.

My mother died when I was eighteen, and one of the aspects I was most troubled by in my grief process was how little the people around me were able to talk about death. And while it's normal for grieving individuals, and the people surrounding them, to want to move forward rather than dwell on the loss, it's inevitable that thoughts of death become more present than ever. How does someone reconcile this experience within a culture that tends to shrink from the idea of death?

I began losing people at a young age. When I was fourteen both

## Preface

of my parents were diagnosed with cancer within months of each other. I was an only child and facing the reality of being on my own in this world before I would even reach adulthood.

So while most of my peers were reveling in a youthful sense of immortality, I found myself asking big questions about life, and what happens when it is over. After my mother died I found myself adrift in a sea of uncertainty. Why did she die? Where did she go? Would I ever see her again? Did I still matter now that the person I mattered most to was gone?

I floundered in this place. I felt a great sense of meaninglessness. I struggled to find purpose in my existence. I worried that at any moment I might die too. I wasn't sure if I should live every day as though it were my last, or if I should be more practical, working and sacrificing to create a solid foundation for a long existence. Most of all, I didn't know whom to turn to with these questions.

I was twenty-five when my father died, and reacting differently than I had with my mother's passing, I worked to embrace his death. I cared for him in his home with the help of a hospice team. I sat with him day after day, fed him by spoon, emptied his catheter bag, and held his hand during our final conversations. I acknowledged that his life had come to an end and that I had to say good-bye.

Losing him was just as painful as losing my mother, but because I had found a way to be present to the end of his life, I did not feel the same guilt and remorse I had following my mother's death. I still yearned to know where he had gone, and if I would ever see him again, and I felt great sorrow and loss over the absence of him in my life. But I knew that I had done everything I could to face this very real truth about life: We will all die.

Following my father's death, I fell into a deep depression for more than a year, and I began to emerge only when I found ways to assign meaning and purpose to my life. I volunteered for a homeless organi-

## Preface

zation. I worked with underprivileged schoolchildren. I went back to school, earned a master's degree in clinical psychology, and began working as a bereavement coordinator for a hospice. I became a wife and a mother.

Yet the question continued to plague me. What happens when we die?

For those of us who do not have some kind of resolute faith or relied-upon religion—a large majority of our younger generations—and even for some of us who do, life after loss can take on a hollow sort of feel. Purpose and meaning are thrown into question and a general anxiety permeates our days. I remember standing in the cereal aisle in the grocery store the week following my father's death, staring at all the brightly colored boxes in front of me. *What is the point of all this?* I kept asking myself.

And while it's true that if we were to spend our lives paralyzed by these philosophical questions there truly would be no point, because we would never get anything done, I do think there needs to be room in our culture to allow for a bigger conversation about death and how it relates to the way we live our lives today.

The idea for this book came to me in the shower, of all places, one day. I was getting ready for a day working with grieving families and I was thinking about my friend Julie, who died of leukemia when we were both in our early twenties. Julie and I had talked openly about death on many occasions during the year she was sick, both of us musing on different ideas we had about what might happen.

Before she died, even though I had never done such a thing, I promised her that I would go to see a psychic medium after she was gone and try to find out if she was okay.

It was a youthful promise, but one that began to nag at me around the ten-year anniversary of her death. That day in the shower, I decided it was time to make good on my promise. And not only

# Preface

that, but to go on a quest to find out more about what happens when we die.

It wasn't just about fulfilling my promise to Julie, but also about quelling this insistent hunger inside me to know more, and to feel more peaceful about death. It was about finding answers not just for myself, but for the people I counsel as well.

Although I began my journey with a visit to a medium, I eventually branched out into many different arenas, including shamanism, past-life regressions, astrology, Judaism, and Buddhism. I knew as soon as I got started that I could probably spend the rest of my life delving into this realm—and I still might—but for the purposes of this book, I simply followed my own interests and the paths that each new experience opened up for me.

When I initially began to foray into the experiences outlined in this book, I struggled to open my mind to them. Countless times I ran up against constructs that had been thrown at me since I was a very young child. Notions of heaven and hell, rules that we must abide by during our lives, and statutes that affect where we go next. I realized that my own grief had been shaped by these messages, and that my feeling of connection to those whom I have lost relied upon the ideas I had in my head about where those people are now.

In order to pursue a new myth, a new belief system, I had to deconstruct my old one, and in doing so I came to understand that this is very much a part of the grief process. We must examine our pre-existing ideas about death in order to find new ones to rely upon. As I embarked on this journey I forced myself to open my mind, and to let go of long-held assumptions, fears, and hopes.

What I found was that the more I explored and the more I let myself ponder it all, the more peaceful I felt, even if certain questions went unanswered. I realized that in allowing myself to ask these questions and to search for the answers, I was finding a way to exist

## Preface

with an uncertainty that I had fought for a long time. And ultimately I realized that fighting the uncertainty was what had caused the anxiety in the first place.

My hope for this book is not to give you a definitive answer about what happens next, but rather to allow you, the reader, to give yourself permission to ask yourself questions you may have been afraid to ask.

My hope for this book is that you close its cover feeling as though death is something to be acknowledged, not ignored, and that you find the same kind of peace I've found, by simply allowing yourself to open up to the uncertainty of it all. We come into this world not knowing what the path before us holds, and we will exit the same way. But just because we don't know doesn't mean we can't explore.

# After This

# Chapter One

I board my flight to New York filled with anxiety. It is the spring of 2011 and I am living in Chicago with my husband, Greg, and our eighteen-month-old daughter, Vera. I kissed them good-bye this morning and climbed shakily into the taxi waiting outside our apartment by the river on Chicago's north side.

I will only be gone for two nights, and it is not the being away from them so much as the mission I am embarking on that is making me nervous. I am on my way to Long Island to meet with psychic medium John Edward.

My visit to John Edward is part of a promise I made to one of my best friends in the last days before she died exactly ten years ago, but it's taken me all this time to get the courage to follow through on it.

Even though I work in the field of death as a hospice bereavement coordinator, I've never seen a psychic medium, never really forayed into the realm of the afterlife. Instead I've worked to help people understand their losses, and to understand my own, through a much more grounded perspective.

I have a master's degree in clinical psychology, something I pursued after losing both parents by the time I was twenty-five. After I had begun to climb out of my own deep grief over those losses, I thought that maybe it would be something I could help others to do as well.

But the work I've been doing in hospice has had much more to do with helping people accept the finality of death, and move forward in their lives without the people who are missing. This work includes leading groups that help people navigate their grief, and I often meet with individuals for one-on-one sessions. In these sessions I work to help people face and accept the absence of their lost loved one. Seeing a psychic medium somehow feels like a betrayal of this.

Yet I find myself filled with a morbid curiosity. Will my dead parents come through? Will my friend Julie come through? Part of me hopes so, but the rest of me would rather they didn't. I'll be left with too many questions if I walk away from this experience thinking that it's possible to communicate with the deceased.

I think about all of this as my flight takes off from O'Hare Airport, winding around the lake toward New York.

After my father died when I was twenty-five, officially leaving me parentless, I stopped thinking about death. I just couldn't. By that time I had lost my mother, my father, and one of my best friends, all within a few years of each other. It was all I could do to get through my days. I barely knew how to be alive, let alone think about what happens when we die.

As much as I want to, I don't feel connected to my lost loved ones anymore. I can't feel them, I can't hear them, and I can't see them. I yearn to believe that they are still around me somehow, looking after me, sending me secret messages from beyond, but I just don't.

Now it feels good to help others along a path I have struggled down myself. It helps me to see death and loss in a more three-dimensional way—to see it not just in terms of my own grief, but in the way my father always urged me to see it, as a larger part of life that we all experience.

And becoming a mother has brought everything even more full circle for me. The night my first daughter emerged from my body in a slick tangle of blood and pain and little outstretched limbs, I recognized something similar in the night my father had died. This coming and going into the world, it is a wondrous thing. I found myself marveling at how much effort we, as a culture, put forth into welcoming a person into the world, and how much we shrink from helping them leave.

In those early days, sitting in the nursery, rocking my tiny daughter to sleep, I thought a lot about Julie, who had died when I was twenty-one. Cradling my newborn in my arms, I wished Julie had been able to experience this part of life. She would have been an incredible mother. The love she would have poured into a child would have truly been something to behold. I struggled to understand why her life had ended so soon.

When my daughter was born I experienced a deeper connection to my parents than I had in years. In an instant, through my own love for Vera, I felt how profound my own parents' love for me had been. Yet even after all the peace I had begun to feel about death being a natural part of life, her tiny existence chipped away at it, making life feel fragile and more uncertain than ever.

I lay awake at night in that first year after she was born, thinking about death incessantly. Ever since my mother died I've been fraught with anxiety about my own mortality. In the first few years after she was gone I was plagued with panic attacks. I couldn't stop worrying that I would die as well—that my heart would just give out, or that I'd get cancer too, or that some horrific accident would befall me. While those fears had eased a bit as I grew older, they began to resurface as I moved into motherhood.

Where would I go if I died? Would I still be able to see my daughter? Would I be able to let her know that I was okay, that she was okay?

I stared up at the ceiling in my darkened bedroom, the little green lights from the baby monitor next to me casting a hazy pallor over the room. I had to find an answer.

A few minutes into my flight to New York to see John Edward, the plane hits turbulence. I clutch the armrests in terror, my heart pounding in my chest. I stare out the window frantically, trying to see the ground below through the pearling clouds. I have only left Vera three times since she was born and each departure has provided me with a new way to worry about something preventing my return to her.

As the plane evens out, my thoughts slow down and they turn to John Edward. I, along with fourteen other people, have an appointment this evening to meet with him, in a hotel conference room on Long Island. Will he have answers for me? I am vehemently skeptical. It just doesn't seem possible. How can someone communicate with the dead? Where are they? Why would they talk to this or that medium specifically?

In the research I've done I know that John Edward McGee, known professionally as John Edward, was born in 1969 on Long Island. The only son of working-class parents, he was raised Roman Catholic. When he was fifteen years old he had a reading by a New Jersey intuitive, who advised him to cultivate his psychic abilities. In my research I've come to understand that intuitives and psychics use paranormal senses to see into a person's past, present, and future. Mediums are those who use these same paranormal senses to also connect with the dead. It is said that all mediums are psychic, but not all psychics are mediums.

## After This

Edward claims that he met this advice with skepticism, but ultimately went on to do just as she had advised. He began conducting psychic readings, and in 1998 his first book, *One Last Time*, was published. Shortly after that he began to host a show on the Sci-Fi Channel called *Crossing Over with John Edward*, in which he gave readings to audience members. Exposure from the show and a growing pop-culture interest in mediums elevated Edward's recognition.

He is currently one of the most well-known psychic mediums in the world, although his abilities have not gone unscathed by criticism, his proclaimed talents having been rebuked by various media outlets and skeptics, as well as independent investigative groups that regularly go after mediums. It does not seem to have affected his popularity or business.

I first heard about John Edward when I was twenty-one years old. I stumbled across *One Last Time* in a shop near my apartment in New York's East Village. My mother had been dead for three years, and Julie was dying. The subtitle of the book, *A Psychic Medium Speaks to Those We Have Loved and Lost*, jumped out at me, and on a whim, I purchased it.

The book fascinated me, even though I had long ago decided that there was nothing after this life. When my mother died I could think only that she was gone and I was never going to see her again.

But something about Edward's book began to push open a crack in a door I thought I'd slammed shut. Suddenly I felt ready to think about life, and death, in a different way. That same month, on a trip to visit Julie in the hospital in Atlanta, I told her about John Edward.

Julie and I had gone to high school together, and had grown particularly close in the years since we'd graduated. She was a bright and luminous person and everyone whom she came into contact with instantly adored her. Just a few months earlier, during her senior year of college at the University of Georgia, she had passed out one day and been rushed to the hospital, where she was diagnosed with acute myeloid leukemia, a strain of cancer rare in someone her age.

News of Julie's illness had hit our friend circle like an atomic shock wave, instantly flattening our youthful feelings of immortality and making us all take stock of our lives. We crowded into the hospital waiting room, paying visits to our beautiful friend while her family and a team of doctors swarmed around her.

On the occasions we had time alone together, Julie and I talked constantly of death. We kept our conversations secret, feeling that we would be admonished if we were to talk openly about the subject.

On one visit I brought John Edward's book with me. I described to Julie the messages Edward claimed to receive, images and symbols from the deceased. For instance, he would see a teapot if you and your loved one had a history of drinking tea together; or a train, or any motif that had featured heavily in the person's life. He claimed these images were confirmation that it was really that person coming through. He even claimed on occasion to have been given secret information about hidden safes or documents that a person had left behind.

Julie and I endlessly pondered this phenomenon of communicating with the dead. *Where* were *the dead people?* we wondered. *And why did they talk to this man?*

Julie had been raised by a Muslim father and a Hindu mother, both born in India. She had traveled there many times throughout her life, enchanted by the myriad differences between that country and the one in which she was raised. She told me long stories about the crowded streets, the cows wandering in between motorbikes, the poverty-stricken children who would press their palms against the windows of the cars she rode in.

For years, each time she had traveled to Mumbai, Julie spent time volunteering at a school for the blind. She told me about how those sightless children had changed everything about the way she saw

## After This

the world. They had made her question what she thought was the purpose of our lives. They made her question God and heaven, and the meaning of everything, in the same ways that I had been beginning to question them.

Julie was afraid to die. She didn't feel ready to let go of her future plans or say good-bye to the people she loved, and I didn't know how to comfort her, other than by simply listening. I desperately didn't want her to die.

One night toward the end of Julie's life my mother came to me in a dream. I rarely dreamt about her, and this visit was so vivid that I sat up in bed in the middle of the night afterward, staring into the darkness for a long time.

In the dream I stood in a windowed anteroom furnished with two chairs and a lamp. I was staring at the door, wondering if I should open it, when my mother appeared.

I immediately broke into sobs, reaching for her. She held me for a moment and then released me. I pleaded with her not to go, and before she slipped through the entryway she turned and said, "I can't stay, honey. I have to see your friend, Julie."

And then the door closed behind her, the dream ending.

The next morning when I got out of bed there was an e-mail from Julie's boyfriend. She'd recently had a stem cell transplant, but scans had just shown that the transplant had not worked. Julie was back in the hospital.

The night I arrived in Atlanta, I found her in her room with another of our high school friends, Channah. They both looked up and smiled when they saw me. "We're planning my funeral!" Julie exclaimed with surreal delight. And Channah nodded at me, smiling through her tears.

I started crying too, a kind of rage building up inside me. All this time I'd been so open to the thought of Julie dying, but now that it was really happening, everything inside me resisted it. I wanted to shout at them to stop. I wanted to pick Julie up in my arms and carry her away from this place. I wanted to stop her death from happening.

But Julie beckoned me to her side and I joined Channah on the bed, listening as they told me about the songs they had chosen for the service.

The next day I stood in the hallway outside her room. Inside were her two younger half sisters, Mary Carson and Kathleen. They were ages seven and nine. They came out holding hands, their eyes wide, the way Julie's would sometimes get.

I walked into the room and took my usual place on the bed at Julie's side. She was crying.

"I just had to say good-bye to them," she said, the tears flowing down her cheeks.

I took her hand. I didn't know what to say. I couldn't think of one single thing that would ease her pain. Julie and I were twenty-one years old and she was dying.

After a few minutes her sobs subsided and she looked at me. "Claire," she whispered. "You know what I'm most afraid of?"

I struggled to come up with an answer. A number of things ran through my mind. A thousand things, in fact.

"I'm afraid that there won't be anyone there on the other side to greet me."

Hearing her say this caused a wave of sorrow to course through me. I shook my head. "Of course there will be," I said, thinking about the dream I'd had about my mother.

"I don't really know anyone who has died," she admitted, her voice wavering.

## After This

"My mom will be there," I said then, some kind of resolute faith rising up through me that this statement was fact.

Julie nodded, looking somewhat satisfied by the response.

"Will you tell her I love her? That I miss her every day?" I asked, tears spilling down onto my shirt.

"Oh, Claire," Julie said. "She already knows."

The next day was Julie's twenty-second birthday. A group of us sat around in the waiting room that morning with flowers and balloons, waiting for Julie to wake up. After a while her mother came in.

"The doctors think she has gone unconscious, that she probably won't wake up anymore."

We took our balloons and flowers into her room anyway, took turns giving her kisses on the forehead as she lay in slumber. Then the group of us found a bar nearby and spent the day there, shaking our heads and toasting to our beautiful friend.

The following afternoon I sat by myself in Julie's room. I had to go home to New York the next morning. My last semester at college was starting and my waitressing job was threatening to disappear if I took any more time off.

It was cold and bright outside and silvery light flooded in through the windows in Julie's room. I sat on the bed and held her hand, watched her chest move up and down with each rasping breath. Her eyes were closed, and I turned her hand over in mine, admiring her long, elegant fingers, trying to memorize them. My tears dripped down onto the bedsheets and I tried to think of some way to say good-bye.

On that last day we'd talked I'd made so many promises to her.

"If I ever have kids, I'll name one of them after you," I'd told her. "And I'm going to write a book about all this one day, I swear."

"Oprah will love it," she'd said, laughing.

"I'll still write you letters too," I said, and she nodded, a smile on her face.

"And I'll read them, wherever I am," she said.

"Oh, and I'll go see John Edward," I told her.

After I had first told Julie about John Edward, we came up with two secret symbols. We vowed never to tell anyone what they were. "If you die," I told her, "I'll go see John Edward and you can come through and tell him those symbols and I'll know you're okay."

"Yes!" she exclaimed. "You have to."

On that last afternoon, sitting in her room, while she lay unconscious, I stared out the window as I held her hand. I knew that even after she was gone, maybe more so than ever, I would continue on my quest to understand what happens when we die.

That night the moon was full and round and I went to sleep, the world feeling large around me. In the morning when I woke up there was a voice mail telling me that Julie had died in the night.

My beautiful friend was gone.

---

Sitting on the airplane, I try to determine my own level of skepticism. When I was packing my suitcase last night my husband jokingly said, "When you see John Edward, ask him where you can buy some snake oil." I laughed, but part of me wondered, *How much do I want to believe in this? And how much will that desire impact my experience?*

John Edward's level of popularity makes it difficult to obtain a private reading with him. His website boasts a lengthy list of events open to the public. Typically held in large venues such as hotel ballrooms and amphitheaters, these events cost $150 to $300 for an individual seat, and are offered throughout the year in places ranging from Orlando, Florida, to Perth, Australia. During these large-scale events he gives random readings to a crowd of hundreds.

## After This

To obtain a private or "small, intimate group" reading, you must sign up on a list through Edward's website and wait to be contacted with further information. Private readings, if you can score one, run $850, and the small group readings cost $650. I suppose I must consider myself one of the lucky ones, as a few weeks prior to boarding this flight I was sitting in front of my laptop when an e-mail popped up from the John Edward wait list, informing me that there were several small group readings being offered in the next month. I had been on the list for several years, but had never actually received an e-mail like this one.

Without hesitation, and knowing that I had only seconds to spare before the reading was sold out, I picked up the phone and reserved a spot for myself. The woman I spoke with told me that I had just booked the twelfth of fifteen spaces. I made the reservation under a false name, using my husband's credit card to hold my booking.

In preparing to research this book and to delve into experiences with psychics and intuitives, I knew that I would need to take precautions to protect my identity, not just for my own need to validate whatever came of the experiences, but in an effort to let readers also feel comfortable that I wasn't being blatantly conned. My first book, a memoir about the loss of my parents, titled *The Rules of Inheritance*, has not yet been published, but I have maintained a blog for many years, writing about my parents' deaths and my grief. It would take just a few simple keystrokes to unearth my identity and a wealth of details about my life.

I know that if I don't strive to protect this knowledge before going into readings, I will always wonder if the information the mediums gleaned just came from a little research on their parts, or if it really came from their psychic abilities. I even go so far as to create a fake e-mail account under the name Phoebe James, and I make a point to pay with cash as often as I can. When I can't pay with cash

I use a credit card with my married surname, not the author name I use online.

———

I land at JFK unscathed, and hop into a taxi to the hotel on Long Island where I am due to meet with Edward in a few hours. I check into the Marriott, feeling more anxious than ever.

I throw my bag on the bed in my room and glance at the clock. I have two hours before the reading. I sit down at the little desk and pull out my notebook. I want to record all of my thoughts before going into this experience.

*Ultimately, I don't believe this guy can contact dead people*, I scribble on the page. *Even if he can, I don't think any of mine will come through.* I think about how I don't have anything outstanding with any of them. There was nothing really left unsaid, nothing yet to be resolved. Wouldn't that be the only reason they would come through?

I write about how one of my biggest fears is for the other people attending this reading. After working in hospice for the past three years, I can't help but imagine the kind of pain people must be in to shell out $650 for a reading with a medium. I can only think that their longing to connect with their lost loved ones must be so great that it eclipses all else in their lives. I worry for their fragile states and I hope that Edward is gentle with them. In fact, in all my experience, I have yet to meet a client who has gone to see a medium. In my mind, it seems to be a choice that must be born out of desperation.

Lastly, I write in my notebook that if anyone does come through, I am hoping it is my mother. Since giving birth to my daughter I have felt incredible pangs of longing for her to know that I am a mother now myself. I have wondered if there is any way she knows this, or if she has seen my beautiful daughter.

## After This

When I checked in a couple of hours earlier I was embarrassed to ask the concierge where the John Edward reading would be held. But he appeared unfazed, answering matter-of-factly, not a trace of the sarcasm or sympathy I expected to hear in his voice. "Just around that corner by the main ballroom," he gestured. "You'll see a sign."

I head in that direction at six forty-five p.m., feeling wobbly as I walk. There is a little table set up outside the small conference room where the reading is to be held, and I check in with a woman holding a clipboard.

"Phoebe James," I tell her, and she scans the list for my name. I hand her an envelope containing $650 in cash, and she counts it out unabashedly before me. There are several people lingering nearby, waiting to see if there are any no-shows for tonight's reading, hoping they'll get a chance to walk into the room I now turn toward.

It's a small room decorated with bland photos of lakes and forests. Two rows of banquet chairs are lined up before a podium. On each chair there is a pen and notepad and a little piece of hard candy wrapped in plastic. I choose a seat in the front row, as close to the far wall as possible. There is one other woman in the room and we offer each other tentative smiles.

Slowly more people begin to file in. A solitary, heavyset man heads to the back row. Two women with perfectly blow-dried hair settle in next to me. They're both wearing expensive-looking shoes and dangly earrings, clutching tiny purses. One of them is pregnant. A handsome man in his thirties joins them, puts his arm around the one who is not pregnant.

A man and a woman, who appear to be father and daughter, join the heavy man in the back row. A gothic-looking woman in her late twenties skirts the edge of the room as she makes her way to the seat behind me. A woman in her sixties, wearing long, flowy hippie garb, stands in the doorway, surveying the room. "I've learned it doesn't matter where you sit with these things," she announces to no one in particular, before flouncing to a front-row seat in direct line with the podium. Two women in their fifties enter, sitting between the gothic woman and the father-daughter duo.

By the time all the seats are filled there are fifteen of us. The man in the father-daughter duo opens up a box of Dunkin' Donuts doughnut holes and offers it around the room. To my surprise there are a couple of takers. The idea of eating doughnut holes in this moment is absurd to me and I almost laugh out loud, but instead I just politely decline when they are passed my way. I am far more nervous than I anticipated. My heart is pounding in my chest.

I think about my daughter and husband back home in Chicago. What am I doing here?

Finally, the woman attendant who collected our payment stands before the podium.

"John will be here in a moment," she says, addressing the room. "Tonight's session will last about two hours, but it may go longer. John will make sure to read every one of you. He talks fast, you guys, so write stuff down. There are pads of paper here and pens if you need them. It tends to get cold in here too, so I hope you all brought a sweater."

I pull my hoodie closer around me, and shift in my seat, trying to get comfortable. I can't decide if I want to be read first or last, or not at all.

Finally, John Edward enters the room with a flourish, and a discernible flutter moves through the rows. People are putting away their phones and doughnut boxes, sitting up straighter in their seats. I cross and uncross my legs, watching as he removes his jacket and takes a swig from a water bottle.

Edward looks just like he does on television—normal, a little tired, almost like a harried father you would see at Disneyland. He rolls up his sleeves, paces around for a minute, and then looks us over. Then he shakes out his arms and cocks his head from side to side. He looks like he's warming up for a track meet, rather than getting ready to commune with dead people.

He starts off right away with the father-daughter duo. "I've got a woman here," he says, gesturing toward the pair. "I feel like she's for you guys, like this is your wife," Edward says to the man who's already nodding. "She's showing me a living room, and, like, a lamp. Is there something funny with this lamp?"

The man is nodding.

Edward continues, his words fast and clipped. "It's like she's telling me that she messes with this lamp. Does she, like, turn it off and on?"

The man is laughing now, and his daughter is holding his hand. "Yeah," he says, "it was this lamp that I bought that she hated, and ever since she died every bulb I put in it goes out within a few days."

Edward is nodding now too, pacing the room even faster. "That's her way of letting you know that she's still with you." He looks around the room, addressing all of us. "This is the kind of stuff they do, guys. They want us to know they're still with us, that they're still connected." The people around me are nodding, and the woman in the father-daughter duo is crying.

He goes on to tell them a few more things—some particulars about the illness the woman died from, her month of birth. "They give me this information to validate their presence," he explains. "This is their way of letting you know it's really them."

It seems like such trivial information to me, birthdates, initials of first names, diseases and ailments. But I guess it makes sense. Nonetheless, I find myself wanting something more concrete.

Finally he gestures to the daughter. "Your mom, she's telling me you have a baby or you're going to have a baby?"

Her eyes grow wide with surprise and she covers her belly with both hands. She stutters as she responds, "Um, uh, I'm only five weeks along," she says. "But no one knows yet."

"Well, your mom knows," John Edward says, and she bursts into tears. I find myself choking up along with her. "She says it's a boy," he continues with a smile.

And then he addresses the room again, tells us a story about how when his wife was pregnant he received a message from one of his own deceased relatives about it before his wife had even taken a test. There are big smiles all around, but I'm tense in my seat.

Is this real? And if so, what does it mean?

Over the next hour he reads another handful of people. The two women in the back who came in together both lost their husbands in an accident when a building exploded. This will go on to be one of the most detailed readings of the night, Edward telling them specifics about the accident and their relationships with their husbands. The women clutch each other, weeping.

"Do you wear one of his shirts to bed?" Edward asks one of them. She nods at him, tears flowing down her cheeks. "Yeah, he's showing me that. He's with you."

"Every night," she says.

The whole room is crying now, including me. I've begun to notice that there's this collective buildup with each person. As Edward begins each new reading everyone leans forward with anticipation, curious to hear this person's story of loss as it unfolds through John's knowledge, all of us seeming to wait for the moment when the connection with the lost loved one seems real. Then the tears flow, a release.

I've never experienced anything like it, and I begin to see why people are drawn to this. There is something therapeutic in this shared grief, in the desperate desire to connect. There is something healing in seeing others find a tiny moment of peace or release from the pain when they feel that connection.

# After This

I hadn't expected to find this kind of therapeutic value in seeing a psychic medium, but now I'm wondering if it shouldn't be considered a more acceptable part of the bereavement process.

By the time John Edward stops in front of me, I'm exhausted. I'm worn out from the release of emotions and grief. I'm overwhelmed by the tragic stories that have come forth: suicides, long illnesses, horrific car accidents. And my whole body has begun to ache from the tension I've been carrying.

Overall, I've been impressed, way more than I expected to be. John Edward seems genuine to me. He's a little cheesy and his manner is kind of abrupt. But he's immersed in this work, obviously committed to it. He makes a lot of jokes, he tells little side stories, and he spends different amounts of time with each person he reads.

It's clear that if he is shamming us, he's not doing it in an obvious way. The details he produces are more specific than not. From time to time he'll offer something and the people he's reading will shake their heads, *No, that birthday, that initial, that illness or teapot or whatever doesn't ring a bell.* But he just continues on, unfazed, until he gets to the thing that makes them sit up in their seat.

At one point while he was reading a woman in the front row he was interrupted by a spirit trying to reach the gothic woman in the back row. "I'm sorry," he said to the woman he'd been working with, "this guy just isn't letting me ignore him." He turns to the woman behind me, telling her he thinks this spirit pestering him is for her.

She shakes her head, says nothing. "Okay, but I really think this guy is for you. Were you engaged or married? He's showing me he's, like, a partner of yours."

She is crying, but refuses to look up, to speak. Edward frowns, cocks his head to the side as though he's listening to something. He shakes his head, glancing at the young woman. "Okay, I'll come back to this in a bit."

He goes back to the woman in the front row, starts to ask her a question, but then stops again, turning back to the gothic woman.

"This guy won't leave me alone," Edward says to her. "James. He's literally yelling the name James at me."

She starts sobbing. "His name was James," she says.

We're all on the edge of our seats at this point. I'm swiveled around in my chair, blatantly staring at her. Mascara is running in rivulets down her cheeks and she's twisting her hands in her lap.

"He's showing me a car wreck," Edward continues. "Oh man, like, it's really mangled. Like, really bad."

She's shivering, nodding, looking down.

"And you were there? You were in the car too?"

She can't speak, won't look up.

"He wants you to know that it wasn't your fault. He's telling me that you think it should have been you? Like, you should have died instead?"

A lot of Edward's statements come off as questions, the person he's talking to nodding when he gets it right.

The woman he's addressing just cries and cries. Finally she speaks. "I . . . I . . . didn't want to be read. I . . . didn't think he would come. I just wanted to be here and listen."

Edward seems unmoved by her tears. "Look, honey," he says. "It doesn't matter if you don't want to be read. This guy is here and he's not going to leave me alone until he gets this message through.

"Here's the thing, guys," he says, addressing all of us. "They don't want us to define our lives by their deaths. If there's one message that comes through more than any other, it's this one. They want you to know that they're still here, they're still connected to you.

## After This

They want you to go on, to live your life, and if they think you're not, well, they're gonna keep pestering me, or you, or anyone who will listen."

I really don't know what to think anymore. The readings are going too fast for me to process my thoughts. I'm jotting it all down in a little notebook on my lap, worried that there will be too much to forget if I don't. I'll just have to think about it all later, figure this out later, I tell myself.

And that's when John Edward finally stops in front of me. Even though he's read most of the room by now, I still feel unprepared when he gets to me.

"Is your grandmother passed?" he starts by asking, and I nod. He cocks his head in that way again, like he's listening. "I've got two women here," he says. "One's definitely your grandmother, and the other is also above you, like, a mother?" I just nod at him.

He looks at me for a moment. "The younger one, the mother one, she's pointing to her hand. 'She's wearing my ring. She's wearing my ring. She's wearing my ring,' she keeps saying. Something about a ring being passed down," he continues, talking rapidly.

I look down at my left hand, at the engagement ring on my finger that once belonged to my mother. "This was her ring," I say quietly.

He nods, unimpressed. "I hate doing jewelry," he says then. "It's so obvious. But she was insistent about this ring."

My heart is racing.

"I've got a man here for you too. He's, like, a little younger than your grandmother but older than your mom, so it doesn't seem like it's your dad, even though that's what he's showing me." Edward is frowning, listening.

"My dad was a lot older than my mom," I say.

"Okay, okay, that makes sense. He's showing me some kind of shoulder pain. Was there something wrong with his shoulder?"

"Um, yeah," I croak. "He dislocated it when he was in his twenties. It always bothered him."

"Yeah, yeah, that's just his way of validating that it's him. Okay, he's showing me, like, this weird story now. It's a story from my life." Edward addresses the room again now. "Sometimes they do this, show me my own memories or stories because they're, like, analogies for something they want the person to know."

"So yeah, he's showing me this story about my friend who threw his kid in the pool when he was little, to teach him to swim. Does that make sense to you?"

"That's pretty much how my dad taught me to swim too," I say, memories of the chlorinated aqua pool at the house I grew up in flooding through me.

"He's trying to use that as a way of saying that's how he parented you. Does that make sense?"

I laugh a little. "Yes. That makes sense."

"And he's giving me a G name. George, maybe?"

"His name was Gerald," I say.

"Right, right. That's what he was telling me. But I wouldn't have guessed that because we already had a Gerald earlier," he says, gesturing to the heavyset man in the back row, whose father also happened to be named Gerald.

After that Edward tries to throw some birthdates at me, the month of February (my grandmother Lulu was born on Valentine's Day), pancreatic cancer (my aunt Jean died of it), the name Nathaniel (my maternal grandfather), but nothing else quite like the messages from my mom about the ring, or my dad and the pool.

And nothing from Julie. Nothing at all. Not a mention of her. Not the symbols we came up with. Nothing.

Abruptly he moves on to a woman seated a few chairs down from me, and just like that my reading is over. I'm too overwhelmed to listen to what John Edward is saying to the woman next to me. I keep staring at the spot to the left of where he is standing, the spot he cocks his head toward when he's listening. Were my mother and father and grandmother standing right there? Were they in this room? Did they see me sitting here in my hoodie with my mother's engagement ring on my finger?

I want to stand up, walk into the space, walk into their arms.

The evening concludes with a question-and-answer session. I am utterly exhausted by this time. Four hours have gone by. I have eaten my hard candy, filled my notebook with pages of scribbles, and sweat through my hoodie, even though I'm somehow still cold.

Edward seems exhausted as well. He has been true to his word, reading everyone in the room. Some of the readings were long and emotional. Others, like mine, short and perfunctory.

I only have one question.

"Where are they? Where are the spirits?"

"Where is the Internet?" he asks me rhetorically. "It exists, right? We use it every day. But we can't see it. We can't put our arms around it."

I nod, trying to twist my thoughts into the logic of this.

"This is just one plane of a multidimensional universe," Edward goes on to explain. "Our sense of time, of space, it's different. Where they are, those things don't matter."

I stare at the floor under my sneakers, trying to understand a place where time and space aren't important.

Edward is gracious with everyone's questions, even though he looks like he's about to pass out. When it's all over I thank him and walk out of the room.

I'm not sure what to do with myself now. I'm tired, but I know I'm too amped up to sleep. I'm walking through the lobby when I spy the two widows heading into the bar. I follow them and ask if I can join them at their table. They nod and I notice that their warm smiles are tinged with a sadness I think must always be there.

We all order stiff drinks. Vodka for me. Gin for them.

"Have you guys done this before?" I ask them.

They look at each other and laugh. Something about them reminds me of my dad and his veteran friends. The bond of having been through something horrific is obvious between them.

"Oh yeah, we've been doing this for a while," they admit.

"Wow," I say, leaning forward. I'm fascinated by the idea of doing this multiple times. "Has it been helpful? Do your husbands always come through?" I have a thousand questions I want to ask, but I try to hold myself back.

"Well," one of them says, stirring her drink with a little red straw. "We saw Allison DuBois last fall and that was amazing." They both nod in agreement. "She really nailed it. Told me more specifics about my husband, about the accident, than anyone ever has."

"That's incredible," I say. "And what about tonight? I mean, that seemed impressive to me." Edward's reading of the two of them was the most detailed of the evening.

"Yeah, yeah, it was good," the other one says. "The thing about the T-shirt? Nobody knows I do that."

"So will you keep going? Are there more mediums you want to see?"

"Oh, I think we're probably done now," says the first one. The other one nods.

"Why is that?" I ask.

"Well, there's only so many times you can hear this stuff. I was really skeptical when we started this whole thing, but now I believe. I've heard enough stuff to really believe," the first one says.

## After This

"Yes, me too," says the one who wears her deceased husband's T-shirt to bed. "But it still doesn't bring them back." Her eyes well up with tears and her friend automatically puts an arm around her.

I lean back in my seat, watching them, these two women steeped in grief.

---

The next day on my flight home, I try to think about it all from my therapeutic point of view.

One of my favorite questions to ask my clients is a simple one: What do you think happens when someone dies? So often, it's been years since they really pondered this question.

When I was earning my master's degree, one of my more memorable classes was a workshop about aging and dying. One afternoon the instructor asked the class to split up into different groups and spend some time sharing with each other our thoughts on what happens when we die.

This exercise was a revelation to me. I couldn't believe we were being given the space and time to do such a thing, and it occurred to me that there really is no place in our lives for conversations like this.

The two other students I was grouped with shared their intimate thoughts about what they thought happens when we die, drawing on their backgrounds and life experiences, and I shared mine. It was a powerful conversation, all of us bringing different perspectives and emotions to the table. They said things I didn't agree with, and other things that made me tilt my head and think about them for weeks following. All of us had constructs we were raised with or taught, and each of us also had life experiences that had altered those constructs. Both of the other students also had ghost stories they wanted to share, tales of inexplicable events following a loss, connections felt or seen yet unexplained.

It was a cathartic conversation for all of us, and I left the class that day feeling profoundly grateful to the instructor who had allowed space for us to have it.

So now I ask my clients to really sit with this question. What do you think happens when we die? I ask them to examine the long-held beliefs they may have, to think about where these beliefs come from and why they hold them. Do they really believe them, or do they feel that they are *supposed* to believe them? Do they fit in with their gut feelings about what happens next?

I encourage them to consider if there are other religious or spiritual beliefs that they have longed to explore. If so, what is holding them back from doing so? I ask them to examine those feelings, to make a list of all the ways they might want to explore the afterlife.

Finally, I ask them if they think it's possible to connect with our lost loved ones, if they have ever experienced a connection, and what that looks like. No matter what I believe personally, my ultimate goal is to help my clients explore their own beliefs, because that is where transformation and healing begin. Finding ways to connect with our lost loved ones is a vital part of the grief process, and it comes in different forms for everyone.

For me it came in the form of writing letters. In the year following my mother's death I struggled to wrap my mind around the idea that I could no longer speak to her. For eighteen years my world had revolved around her. There was nothing I had done that she did not know about, no decision I made for which I did not seek her counsel. But suddenly she was gone and I longed to continue communicating with her.

At the one-year mark of her death I'd had enough. I couldn't bear it anymore and so I sat down and wrote her a letter. At that time I didn't believe in God, or an afterlife, but it didn't matter. I needed to talk to my mom.

## After This

So I wrote and I wrote. I told her about all the things that I'd done in the year she'd been gone. I wrote about the grief that had consumed me, the adventures I'd been on. I described my evolving relationship with my father in her absence, and even anecdotes about our pets, whom she had dearly loved.

It felt so good to write to her—to not just think about her and wish she were there to see these things, but to actually write directly to her, as though she could read the things I wrote about. In fact, it felt like she could. Although I cried throughout the entirety of writing the letter, I also felt a great weight lift as I wrote.

She's now been gone for half of my life, and I still write her letters every year on the anniversary of her death. In fact, this is now the foremost exercise I urge my clients to do when they are steeped in grief and longing for a connection with their loved one.

It's not just that we want to know that our loved ones are okay. We want them to know that we are okay as well. We want them to know how much we loved them, how much we miss them.

Without fail, every time I have asked clients what they would say to their loved ones if they had the chance, it's always the same message.

"I'd want them to know that I love them. That I miss them. That I think about them every day."

Sometimes there are lengthier messages—regrets expressed, life updates, questions. But they always begin with the same yearning to have the loved ones know how much they are missed.

And this is exactly what I saw occurring in the reading with John Edward. Every single person in that room wanted just those things. They wanted to know that their loved ones were okay, and they wanted to know that they were still connected.

I replay the reading over and over in my head. I stare out the window at the sky and clouds and when the plane hits a few bumps I don't even flinch. I'm too lost in thought.

### Claire Bidwell Smith

I think about all those letters I've written my mother, all the things I've told her about—graduating college, earning a master's degree, moving across the country several times, getting married, giving birth to my daughter. All the things I wish she could have been here to see.

After my reading with John Edward, now I'm wondering if it's possible that she has been here all along.

# After This

Dear Vera and Jules,

It's a Wednesday morning and I just dropped you both off at school together, then came home to take a call from a new client who recently lost her mother. This forty-year-old woman wept into the phone as she described the hole that has been left in her life now that her mother is gone.

I could feel my own throat closing up as her soft cries filled the earpiece, and I immediately thought about both of you, hoping that you never find yourself making such a phone call, that you're never grieving the loss of your mother, yet knowing that you surely will one day.

I'm writing you these letters for just that reason. I know they won't be the same as having me here in the flesh, but they'll be something one day if you need them. Mother loss permeates my life, both personally and professionally, and from the moment I became a mother myself, my biggest fear has been that I will leave you too soon.

So I'm writing these letters now, when you are just two and five years old, in case I'm not here when you are twelve or sixteen or twenty-five or thirty-six. There are things I want to be able to talk to you about, to explain, to impart, and so I will do my best to put them all down here.

I've actually been writing to you since before you were born. I always knew I would have daughters. I knew, after my mother died, that somehow the mother-daughter relationship would come back around in my life, and I've been preparing for it for so long.

I wrote the first letter to you when I was twenty-four years old. I was living in Manhattan in a five-floor walk-up in the East Village. My mother had been gone for six years and I had become entrenched in a terrible relationship with a young man who was just as troubled as I was. We were both lost and scared and afraid to be on our own in the world, and so we clung to each other in all the worst ways possible.

One night we got into an argument and I fled the apartment. I had the keys to a friend's place down the street—I was feeding her cat while she was out of town—and I still remember walking tearfully past Tompkins Square Park in the dusk to her apartment. I sat in her little studio at a desk, and wrote out a letter to my unborn daughters.

*Don't ever find yourself in this place,* I wrote. *Don't ever be so afraid of the world, or so destroyed by grief, that you let someone else control you.*

I've since lost the letter, but I still remember those lines.

Sometimes I just can't believe that loss can destroy a person so much, but as I listened to that client on the phone this morning I was reminded that it can. Yet still, I wonder, how is it possible that loss, such an inevitable part of our lives, can be this hard to grapple with?

I think I've been on a quest all these years to find an answer to that question. That's what this book is about, what these letters are about.

I suppose that when you love someone as much as I

love you, and as much as you love me, it's only fair that the absence of that person is this enormous. It wasn't until I became a mother myself that I finally saw it all so clearly. I never quite understood why her death had been so hard on me until you were born. And then in a flash I understood it.

As I held each of your tiny bodies in my arms, as I fed you and bathed you and rocked you to sleep, and poured more love than I thought possible into you, I was flooded with the impact of the bond I had shared with my own mother. All of those forgotten years, the early ones, when the relationship is so symbiotic, had been forgotten by me as I grew older, but nonetheless they had laid the foundation for my love and deep attachment to her.

When she was gone, so too was the sense of being anchored in this world. Gone was the person who knew me better than I did. Gone was the person who believed in me more than anyone else ever will. And gone was the person who was supposed to be there each time I looked back, as I ventured into the world on my own.

What I couldn't understand for a long time was that she was still here. What I couldn't understand was that I will always have an internal mother, one built out of her love for me, and out of the ways in which she taught me what nurturing looks like. I'm teaching you these things as we speak, helping you build your own internal sense of mother.

You may not remember the specific ways in which I held you or sang to you, or taught you how to bake cakes, but they'll live on inside you anyway, and you'll know what they feel like, even if I'm not here to remind you.

## Claire Bidwell Smith

I want you to know that love never dies, girls. My love for you, in the very moments you were born, was already so great that it eclipsed anything else I have ever felt in my life. It would be impossible to destroy it, regardless of any vast physical distance in death or life that could come between us.

All you have to do is close your eyes and let yourself feel it.

Love,

*Mom*

# Chapter Two

Back home in Chicago I hold Vera in my arms as she falls asleep one afternoon. She is almost two years old at this point, but I still like rocking her to sleep. I stare down at her perfect face, the skin smooth and unlined, her gentle eyelashes resting against her cheeks in slumber. Her chest moves up and down and her body is warm in my arms.

I'm still turning over the experience with John Edward in my head, but over the next few weeks, life returns to normal. I wake each morning next to my husband, get up, make coffee, feed Vera, and get dressed for work. When the nanny arrives I get in my car and head out into the snowy Chicago suburbs, driving around to various homes where people are caring for their dying loved ones.

Each time I walk into one of these houses with my heavy bag full of folders and grief handouts, I am reminded of the days I spent caring for my father. I sit at the bedsides of unconscious people I have never met while their sons or daughters tell me the details of their lives.

One morning I meet with a woman in her thirties whose husband is actively dying. They have a three-year-old daughter, and she cries to me at the kitchen table about how she does not know how she will go on to raise her daughter without him. I want to reassure her, to tell her that she will be able to assume this task no matter how insurmountable it may feel in this moment, but I know that right now she simply needs to grieve the life she once thought she was going to live. I hold her hand, this woman whom I have only just met, and I let her cry.

Back in my car, I watch tiny snowflakes land on the windshield and I forget to accelerate when the traffic lights turn green.

What are we doing here? What is the purpose of all this? What happens after this?

Each night, putting Vera to sleep, I think about what it is I want her to know about life, what I might want to leave behind for her.

---

A few weeks after my visit to John Edward I start to feel this itch. It wasn't enough, I realize. I want to see another medium.

I decide I don't want to see another big one like John Edward. I'm curious to talk with someone one-on-one. And I want to see someone who isn't so full of hype. A simple Google search of psychic mediums in Chicago leads me to a woman named Delphina in Irving Park.

Using my fake e-mail account, I send her a note, requesting a session. She responds the next day and says she'd like to chat by phone first. She informs me that she screens all her potential clients to make sure they are in a good place with their grief process. I call her from a blocked number and we chat for a few minutes.

Delphina wants to know how far out I am from my loss. I tell her it's been a matter of years and that I'm in a good place, that I'm just curious about seeing a medium.

Her voice is kind, and I like that she doesn't take just anyone on, that she acknowledges the importance of the grief process. I know from experience the desperation some people can feel in their grief, and that it's an emotion that needs to be handled carefully.

A few days later I find myself driving down Irving Park Road, approaching the blinking dot on my phone's map where her modest office is located. I find myself nervous again. I realize that I am wanting so much more from this visit than the one I had with John Edward.

I just want more. I want more of my mother. I want more of my father. I want Julie to come through. But with that desire comes anxiety. I have to admit to myself that there is a spooky element to all of this, and it makes me nervous. What kind of door am I opening, and to what?

As an adolescent I was always drawn to the occult. When I was in the seventh grade and just beginning to write my first poems, I memorized Edgar Allan Poe's "The Raven." I recited it to my parents at dinner one night, leaving them both flabbergasted.

> *Deep into that darkness peering, long I stood there wondering, fearing,*
> *Doubting, dreaming dreams no mortal ever dared to dream before*

I'd always been a weird kid, lonely and thoughtful, disappearing for long hours into books or my playroom, where I dreamed up whole worlds and lives for my dolls and toys. I think it was partly the only child's plight, the solitary world I was forced to inhabit. But for as long as I can remember I've been curious about the meaning of life, watching it unfold with a kind of existential slant, before I even knew the definition of *existential*.

Maybe it had to do with my father's advanced age, his constant musings at the dinner table on life and the unexpected places it takes us. He had been a bomber pilot in WWII, shot down over Czechoslovakia in 1944 on his way to bomb Hitler's remaining oil refineries in Germany. He had parachuted out of a burning plane, been captured by the Germans, and survived the prison camp on bread made of sawdust for six months, until the war ended. His view on life was a unique one, and he often waxed philosophical on the meaning of it all.

My mother, by contrast, was full of energy and creativity. She was an artist, and lived life messily, impulsively. She taught me how to use my imagination, convincing me that fairies were real, that my dreams were to be paid attention to, that nature and all its creatures were to be revered. She liked the idea of magic, the concept of transformation. She was an alchemist, turning a blank page into a beautiful picture, a pile of ingredients into a cake. She liked to ponder the potential of everything.

Although their approaches to life were a little different, my mother and father both contained the same element of possibility. Neither of them was deterred by the usual barriers that seem to adhere most people to a conventional life, and because of this, life always seemed a little surreal to me.

It was as if there were a closed set of curtains, and if I could just find the opening, I could reveal an entirely different world than what appeared before me. By the time I was in high school I was lighting candles and burning incense, reading books about witchcraft and lucid dreaming. I wanted to believe in magic, in the possibility of more than what lay before me.

But sitting here in my car, on Irving Park Road, about to see a psychic medium, I realize how far away from those notions I've strayed. As I grew older the world set in around me, logic and practicality, rules and standards edging out all the magic of my youth. My parents' deaths made life seem filled with impossibility, rather than possibility. I long ago stopped believing that there was more.

I find myself apprehensive about this door I'm pushing open again, partly because I'm not sure what I'm toying with, and in what ways it will threaten the stable view of life I've created for myself, and partly because I fear that I will want more than it can give me.

---

Delphina is in her early forties. She has warm brown eyes and messy hair. Her clothes are simple and her office is small and cluttered. It's a windowless space in the back of a nondescript brick building. There are two chairs set up, incense burning, candles everywhere.

"Hi. My name isn't really Phoebe," I say immediately. "It's Claire. I was just worried about preserving my anonymity before the session."

She just looks at me for a minute, and then nods. "Yes," she says. "I thought something was off when you told me that was your name."

She gestures to one of the chairs. "Have a seat. You said you've done this before? You've seen a medium?"

"Yeah, a couple of weeks ago. I saw John Edward."

"Oh yeah? How was that?" She doesn't seem particularly impressed; rather, just curious.

"It was okay. It was with a group of people. I'm looking forward to doing this one-on-one," I tell her. She nods at me and takes a seat across from the chair I'm sitting in.

"Okay," she says, settling into her chair, "the reading will last about an hour. You can ask me any questions you want and I'll try to be as clear as possible with my answers. To begin, I need something of yours to hold, some kind of personal belonging."

I'm not sure what to give her. My pockets are empty; the objects in my purse aren't very personal. I settle on my engagement ring, the one that belonged to my mother, as John Edward pointed out. I slip it off my finger and pass it across to her. Delphina takes it in her hands and begins to rub it back and forth between her fingers, closing her eyes.

"Please state your full name out loud three times."

I pause for a moment, unsure if I should say my legal married name or the name I was given at birth. I decide on my maiden.

"Claire Bidwell Smith. Claire Bidwell Smith. Claire Bidwell Smith."

My name feels funny in my mouth, saying it three times like this. Bidwell is my middle name, passed down from my great-grandfather on my mother's side. As a kid I hated it, envying my friends with their pretty middle names like Elizabeth or Grace. But now as an adult, I've grown to like it.

The room is quiet now, my voice having dissipated into the air, and Delphina sits with her eyes closed, holding my ring. I'm unsure of what to do. I feel uncomfortable watching her, but I'm too nervous to close my own eyes. I stare down at my hands in my lap. I am aware of her motion from the corner of my eye. She shivers and twitches a bit, cocking her head from side to side and occasionally using one of her hands to push away at the air around her, as though she is removing invisible objects from the surrounding space.

Finally she speaks. "There is a man here. He died of a massive heart problem. Too soon. Too fast. He wasn't ready."

I frown a bit, unsure of who this could be. It's definitely not my father. "Um, I'm not sure," I say.

"He's very tall, maybe in his fifties. Funny, kind of a goofy guy."

I'm silent, thinking about who it could be.

"He says he's your brother."

"Eric," I say to Delphina. "He was my half brother."

I am immediately filled with guilt for not thinking of him sooner. Eric was my father's youngest child from his first marriage. My father had married a woman named Helen in his early twenties, just before he went off to war. They had three children together, my half siblings. By the time my father met and married my mother all three of them were in their thirties. They have always been part of my life, but rather than feeling like siblings, they've seemed much more like aunts and uncles.

Five years ago Eric had a massive heart attack, at age fifty-six. He was found by his new wife dead on the floor of my half sister's basement, where he was living. Although I was somewhat close to him, I hate to admit that I rarely think of him now, and certainly didn't expect to hear from him today.

"My half brother," I say again.

Delphina shakes her head. "He says no, that you were always his sister."

I feel another rush of guilt, and one of gratitude. Tears spring into my eyes, and I nod. Maybe we hadn't shared a bedroom growing up, or fought over toys, or gone to the same schools, but we did share the experience of being fathered by the same man. I nod again and Delphina continues.

"He's showing me a woman, his wife? He wants you to know how grateful he is to you for being there for her after he died."

I'm floored. How could she know these things? I can't even speak, but Delphina can tell that what she's saying is resonating.

Eric lived a troubled life. He'd never quite found his place in the scheme of things, as our father always put it. As a kid he'd always gotten into trouble. He ran away from home, skipped school often, flunked out of college. In his thirties he worked for our father's company, but their relationship had been a contentious one, Eric never feeling comfortable taking direction from our dad.

By the time he was in his forties (my high school years) he'd retreated to a solitary cabin in the woods of Mississippi. He lived there for many years, alone with his dog and his vast collection of blues records. He smoked two packs of Camels every day, finished each night with a case of Budweiser. We all worried about him. Finally, at the end of our father's life, Eric left Mississippi and moved in with my half sister Candace in the suburbs of Virginia.

Everyone in our family felt relieved that Eric had come out of his hermitage, but I'm not convinced that it was the best thing for him. I think he'd been happy there in the woods with his dog and his smokes and his thoughts. Living in my half sister's basement with a job as a courier seemed to make him miserable.

After our father died, Eric took his small inheritance from the sale of Dad's condo and went to Thailand. He met a woman there named Tim, who would become his wife. While they worked on her visa application, he lived with her family in their small village outside Bangkok. Eric had always been a handy guy, and he repaired their plumbing system, installed a new roof on their house, and paid for her three young daughters to see the eye doctor. They all needed glasses.

Eventually Tim's visa came through and she moved to Arlington, Virginia, to live with Eric in Candace's basement. I can't imagine what that life must have been like for her. She spoke very little English, had left her daughters behind, and spent her days riding shotgun in Eric's pickup truck as he made his courier deliveries.

One afternoon, only a few months after her arrival in the United States, Tim walked downstairs to find Eric dead on the floor. The following weekend, when I arrived for the funeral, I let Tim stay in my hotel room with me. She curled into a corner of the bed and wept and wept, trying in her broken English to explain the trauma of it all. I put my arms around her and let her cry. I had no idea what to do for her. I was twenty-seven years old.

My half sister urged Tim to return to Thailand. Candace was too

## After This

overwhelmed by her own life to take on this newly immigrated woman. But Tim had only just arrived here and was reluctant to give up what she thought might be a better opportunity for her family in the future. She asked if she could live with me, in California, and I tried to imagine her in my one-bedroom apartment in Venice Beach.

Ultimately, Tim moved in with a Thai family in Virginia. I've stayed in touch with her all these years, sending her money when I can, and doing my best to make her feel still connected to our family. It's never seemed like enough, though, and I've often wondered if I should have brought her to California with me after Eric died.

All of this rushes over me as Delphina continues to speak. "He's very clear about this. He's showing me over and over that he really wants you to know how grateful he is that you were there for this woman. He worries about her, about her children. He wants you to know how much it means to him that you were there for her."

I'm shaking all over. I simply cannot fathom how Delphina could know these things, unless she's really talking to Eric. I just keep nodding at her. She's looking to my right as she talks, as though Eric is standing there. I turn my head and look at the empty space.

Delphina laughs. "He was a funny guy, wasn't he? Like, a trickster?"

I nod and smile. Eric was goofy, always playing jokes and pranks. He was always teaching me riddles and teasing me into believing some fantastic story. He was odd too. At one point he had a skunk for a pet. And in the eighties he had a DeLorean, taking me for a drive one afternoon around the neighborhood with the doors opened up to the sky.

I'm still musing on Eric's life, my complicated relationship with him, and his untimely death when Delphina continues.

"There's another man here with him now. I believe it's your father. He's older. He's showing me breathing problems, lung stuff, heart stuff."

My father was on oxygen at the end of his life. He had contracted tuberculosis in the prison camp, and he suffered from emphysema after years of smoking. During his last few years he had to carry an oxygen tank with him. He also had heart problems, having a stent installed just a year before he died.

I nod at her again. I'm amazed at her specificity. I've told her nothing about whom I've lost in my life. I have not mentioned my mother or father or Julie.

Her eyes are closed again and she's taking deep breaths. "He's showing me how close you were, how much gratitude he had for you being there for him at the end."

I'm really crying now, pulling my arms around myself. Is my father really here, in this room with me right now?

"He's showing me that you took care of him? Like a nurse?" Delphina asks.

I nod, and images of those last weeks with him in a hospital bed in his condo wash over me.

"He's really grateful for that time you had together, he's saying. He loves you so much."

I just nod. I'm too overcome with emotion to speak. All I wanted in those last days of my father's life was for him to understand how much I loved him.

"He's showing me a child now, very little. A girl? Do you have a daughter?" Delphina asks, opening her eyes.

I nod, again in surprise. Obviously I'm married. She can tell that by the ring I handed her. And I'm of childbearing age, but again, I've said nothing about being a mother.

"He's telling me he's with her a lot. Oh, he loves her. He's with her all the time," she says.

I think about Veronica, the idea of my father knowing she exists, the idea of him actually being with her. It's almost too much to process. I continue to tremble. Delphina tells me more things about him, making me believe even more that she is really communicating with him. She describes his height (he was six feet five) and his birth month (October), his mathematical mind (he was an engineer) and his good-natured humor.

She grows quiet again, rubbing her fingers over my ring, taking more deep breaths. From time to time she pulls at the air around her, and occasionally a shudder goes through her. She cocks her head again.

"Your mother is passed as well?" she asks, opening her eyes to look at me, and I nod. She closes them again. "She's here now too. She's shy," she continues, "but that seems weird to me. Like she was not shy in life."

I laugh a little. "She definitely wasn't shy," I say. My mother was the opposite, in fact. Glamorous and charismatic, she commanded every room she entered.

I can only remember her being shy once. It was the year before she died. She came to visit me for parents' weekend at the college I had just begun attending in Vermont. A couple of months before, the fall after my senior year of high school, she and my father had driven me up to the small liberal arts school I had chosen. My father put together a bookshelf and my mother helped me to fit flannel sheets over the twin bed in my dorm room.

When they drove away at the close of that weekend I waved at their car all the way down the long road from school, until it took a turn and I could no longer see them. I returned then to my dorm room and my new friends, both thrilled and terrified by the start of my new life.

Six weeks later my mother returned by herself to visit me for parents' weekend. It had been the longest we'd ever been apart. We had written letters and spoken on the phone frequently during those six weeks. She had sent care packages every week packed full of magazines and homemade brownies, which I had devoured on my bed, hungry for the taste of home.

I remember watching her car pull up in front of my dorm that October weekend. I watched her step out, shielding her face with her hand to obscure the late-afternoon sun. She had cut her hair short since I'd last seen her, and when she got close to me we stood for a moment, awkwardly taking each other in before we embraced. It struck me in that moment, all those years ago, that she felt shy standing there before her daughter, who had so newly stepped into the world without her.

I think about this now, sitting in Delphina's tiny office in Chicago, and in that sense, I can imagine my mother shy again, approaching her now-grown daughter, who has become a woman and a mother, who has gone on to live her life in her absence.

"She's showing me lower abdominal problems. Intestinal stuff. All kinds of problems, pain, a surgery?"

I nod. "She had colon cancer."

"She's apologizing for leaving you too soon," Delphina says then, and I begin to cry again. "She wants you to know that their lives are not yours. That you are going to be okay. That you *are* okay."

I nod some more, looking down at my hands, thinking about my fear of leaving my own daughter prematurely.

"She doesn't want you to worry so much," Delphina says, and then she grows quiet again for a while.

"Oh, she's proud of you," she says. "She says you're an artist."

"No, no," I say. "She was an artist."

"Yes, she's showing me that, but she says you're an artist too. She says you're pragmatic, though." Delphina continues to rub my ring. Her eyes are closed again and she takes another deep breath. "She's showing me books, writing. You wrote a book?" she asks, opening her eyes.

## After This

I nod. I have just completed my first book, The Rules of Inheritance. Just a few weeks before, I sent the final draft to my editor at Penguin, and this week I will begin to work on the edits she has for me. "Yes, I have a book coming out next year," I say. "It's about my parents."

Delphina nods. "Your mom is showing me another book, though, too. You're working on another book?"

"I am," I say. "It's why I'm here. It's about the afterlife."

Delphina nods, closes her eyes again. "She's so proud of you," she says about my mother. "She's telling me that you come from a long line of artists and writers, and she's just so happy that you're actually successful, that you're making money."

The entirety of my mother's family comprises creative people. My aunts and cousins are all artists and writers and musicians. We even have a few famous people in our lineage. Both Washington Irving and the English poet Thomas Chatterton are my ancestors.

"She's just so proud of you," Delphina says again.

I smile. Of course my mother would say that. She took pride in my accomplishments to a point that was embarrassing, always touting my modest achievements to her friends, and having more confidence in my abilities than I ever had in myself. She loved that I was a writer, and was always encouraging me to share my poems with her. In high school I often woke her up in the middle of the night to read her something I'd just written.

She'd sit up in bed, blinking as she switched on the bedside lamp, smoothing the sheets next to her so that I could sit down. "Okay, I'm ready," she'd say, rubbing the sleep out of her eyes and settling in to hear my new verses, even though it was past one in the morning.

"Oh, honey," she'd say when I was finished. "I'm so proud of you."

When I was done reading I'd tuck her back in and give her a kiss on the cheek before she'd turn off the light and go back to sleep. In the morning she'd always ask to hear the poem again. For these past thirteen years I've missed her enthusiasm for my pursuits fiercely.

"She's showing me a painting. Maybe it's something she did? It's kind of abstract, bright colors, strong shapes. She's showing me a vision of you sitting beneath it, writing," Delphina says.

I flash to our dining room table in Chicago, where I've been sitting for months as I work on my memoir. Just to the right of it on the wall hangs a painting my mother did in college. It's a cityscape at night, all angles and abstract shapes, bright colors, just as Delphina described.

I tell this to Delphina and she nods at me. "Yes, she's with you when you're writing. That's why she's showing me this. She wants you to know that."

I shake my head, in disbelief that this woman is telling me all these things about my life, all these things she couldn't possibly know.

"She's telling me she's with you and your daughter a lot too," Delphina continues. "She's showing me butterflies?"

"Butterflies?"

"Yes," she says. "Colorful butterflies. Something about butterflies and your daughter."

I shake my head. I don't yet have any association with butterflies.

"She just keeps showing me these butterflies. She's so insistent about them and your daughter."

"Oh, god," I say as it suddenly dawns on me. I pull up the sleeve of my sweater. On my forearm a colorful swarm of butterflies arcs upward toward my elbow. It's a temporary tattoo my daughter Veronica insisted I place there to mimic the one on her arm. We gave them to each other earlier that week.

Delphina and I both look down at my arm and she laughs. "Yes, that's what she was showing me."

My sweater is a heavy, fitted one; it's still winter in Chicago. I'm positive that Delphina couldn't have seen the tattoo before this moment. I shake my head, feeling stunned by everything that has transpired in this past hour.

"They're always with you, your parents," she says then.

"But where?" I ask, a desperate pleading in my voice. "Where are they?"

"They're here. They're there. Parts of them are always with us. It's the 'collective all.' We're all connected, even in death. Acknowledge them," she says. "Keep them with you. Put pictures of them up. Talk to them. They're with you."

When I leave Delphina's office I'm in a daze. It's the middle of the day in Chicago, one of the last bright, cold days before spring finally begins to show itself. I stand on the street looking out at the world around me, cars driving by, snow in heaps on the ground.

I can't bring myself to go home just yet, so I make my way across the street to a Starbucks. It's warm inside and bustling. I order a latte and take a seat at a little table, pulling out my laptop to furiously write out notes from the session I just had. From time to time I look up at the people around me, all of them coming and going so busily, so immersed in their lives.

What *is* all this? What are we doing?

I remember that sense when I was younger, of feeling as though I could pull aside some curtain and see another world before me. Everything in this moment looks different. The curtain has shifted.

I lean back in my chair, trying to sort through my thoughts.

Am I being scammed? Am I so emotional, so desperate to hear from my parents that I am simply believing anything these mediums say?

I don't think that's the case. I have gone into each of these sessions feeling levelheaded, not *needing* to hear anything. The connection to Eric was especially surprising. I wasn't expecting to hear anything from him, wasn't even thinking about him.

The details Delphina brought forth about each of the three were so specific. I never once felt as though she were leading me on or digging for information. Even more so than John Edward, who moved so quickly and turned most of his statements into questions, Delphina seemed to just present exactly the information she was receiving.

Maybe she was reading my mind, I think then. But even so, that's kind of phenomenal, right?

---

Over the next few weeks I monitor my emotional state following the reading with Delphina. I still haven't determined whether I think it was real, but I do know that I have a new sense of peace. Something inside me feels softer.

I have opened myself to the possibility that I am still connected to my parents, that they are with me in my life, that they know my daughter, my husband, my world. Just the idea of that possibility makes things feel different. The starkness of the world has lessened.

Both personally and in my profession, I've found that the biggest struggle with grief lies in how much we hold on to the people we love. Our culture implores us to let go, to move on, and I think many people struggle in the face of this message.

I've heard countless widows and widowers tell me that the people in their lives have urged them to remove their deceased spouse's belongings from the house, to begin dating again, to work at creating a new life without that person. This is easier said than done. The people who say these things mean well. They want to see us happy again, and it makes them sad and fearful to see someone struggling with the intense emotions that come with grief.

## After This

So often bereaved people listen to these messages. Either they follow through with them, removing most traces of their deceased loved one, yet continuing to feel that gaping absence; or they keep things around, continuing to act and feel connected to their lost person, yet feeling guilty for doing so.

My experience so far with mediums has been one that has reinforced the notion that we need to continue to feel connected to our lost loved ones. We need to keep them in our lives. Whether that is by simply keeping photos around, talking about them to our friends and family, or fully believing that we are indeed connected, as the mediums suggest, it seems to me that this is a healthier way to grieve our losses rather than trying to move on completely.

After my visit to Delphina, I feel a renewed determination to embrace my parents' presence in my life, whether or not I believe that I am still connected to them on a spiritual level. For years I have struggled with how much to hold on to or let go of them. Finally, it is beginning to make sense to me that I can move forward with my own life, yet still feel love for them, still honor their existence in my life.

I know that to fully believe my experiences with Delphina and John Edward were real, to believe that they were truly connecting with my dead parents in an afterlife, would require a certain amount of faith on my part.

For weeks after seeing Delphina I chew on this notion of faith. What is it? And how can I find some?

A couple of years from now I find myself reflecting on my visits to Delphina and John Edward before I'm headed off on another trip. The night before leaving I lie in bed with Vera, coaxing her to sleep. "Mama," she says suddenly, "I'm going to miss you."

"I know, baby," I reply, feeling my own emotions rise to the surface. I always feel especially sensitive to the idea of her missing me, knowing all too well what it is like to miss my own mother.

"Here's the thing," I tell her. "Even when we're not together, we still are. Anytime we're apart, all you have to do is close your eyes and think about me. Concentrate on the feeling in your heart, on your love for me, and let yourself feel how much I love you back. You can even send me messages. You can talk to me in your head, and I'll hear you."

The words are out of my mouth before I really have time to process them. I'm not even sure if I believe what I'm telling her, but I know that I want her to believe.

She stares at me wide-eyed. "Really?"

"Sure," I say, thinking about the letters I write to my mother and how it always feels like she can hear me. "No matter how far apart we ever are, all you have to do is close your eyes and tune in to me and I'll be there."

"Can we try it right now?" Vera asks.

"Okay," I reply a little hesitantly.

We both close our eyes. I can feel her little body snuggled up next to me in bed, her breaths quick and childlike.

"Okay," she whispers after a minute. "What message am I sending you?"

I crack one eye open and look at her. Her eyes are still closed, but I can tell that she is concentrating. I close my eyes again, smiling. "You're telling me that you love me."

"Mama!" she exclaims, sitting up in bed. I open my eyes and sit up too. "How did you know?" she asks incredulously.

The truthful answer is that she is a toddler, and there aren't a lot of complex messages that she could be sending me. But an even more truthful answer is the one I give her. "I could just feel it," I say.

She smiles back at me and lies back down beside me. Within a few minutes she is asleep. I lie there for a while beside her, thinking about the exercise we just did. It was simple, but I often let my head get in the way of such acts. I smile again, though, thinking about her

# After This

sending me messages the following week while I am away, knowing that after this she'll really believe I'm receiving them.

And in a way, I feel like I will. But more important, she will feel free to send me love, rather than pine for me and miss me, which is something I'm only now learning to do with the people I miss.

I can feel something in me shifting, something about my willingness to let myself feel connected to my parents even though they are gone. I begin to bring it up with my clients, asking them about the ways they feel connected or not to their loved ones.

One client tells me about how she always feels close to her mother when she is cooking and gardening. Another tells me that he feels completely blocked when he tries to imagine that he is somehow still connected to his dead father.

"What would it be like to even just pretend you're connected?" I ask them. "What would that feel like? What would it look like?" I suggest writing letters, placing more photos of their loved ones around the house. I also suggest talking to them, either out loud or in their heads.

Watching Vera's reaction to our little exercise that night made me realize that even if we don't fully believe we are connecting in these mystical ways, it is worth something to *feel* like we are.

Maybe this is what it means to have faith.

# Claire Bidwell Smith

Dear Vera and Jules,

All these experiences have reminded me of just how rigid we can become as adults. When we are children it is easy to believe in magic. It's easy to break rules or disregard them, or to seek out alternative truths.

But something happens as we age, and life begins to pigeonhole us into a rigidity that isn't always necessary. As we grow older we are taught endlessly about what is acceptable and what is not, and there is a tendency to forget how to marvel in just how magical life can be. My mother had always been diligent in her efforts to teach me exactly this kind of magic, but after she was gone I think I lost it for a while. You girls have brought it back to me in a thousand ways.

The other morning as we exited the back door, on our way to the garage so that I could drive you to school, Jules, you stopped because you found a dead beetle hanging in a spiderweb underneath the railing of the stairs.

"Mom, Mom, a beetle!" you cried.

I was feeling rushed because we were late, as usual, to preschool drop-off, and my arms were laden with lunch bags and car keys and sunglasses, but you were insistent that I take a look at this beetle.

I doubled back and squatted down beside you, and Vera, you joined us, and together we all peered at the beetle. It was a little thing, rust brown in color, its legs protracted in its final position, swinging in the light breeze under the stairway.

## After This

Jules, you wrapped your arms around yourself with anxiety. "I scared, Mama," you said.

"It's dead!" Vera yelled.

"It is dead," I told you both. "But there's nothing to be afraid of. It can't hurt you. Even if it were alive it wouldn't hurt you," I said.

"It's not real," you said, Jules.

"No, it is real. It's dead, though. It won't move anymore," I replied.

You both stared at it a while longer and finally I stood up. "Let's get to school, girls," I said. You turned away from the beetle and followed me like little ducklings to the garage.

That afternoon, returning from school, Jules, you started talking about the beetle again before we were even home.

"I want to see it again, Mama," you said.

"Okay, let's check on it on our way inside," I said.

We stopped again at the stairway before going into the house, and the beetle was still there, swinging in the breeze.

"I not scared, Mama," you said, looking at it.

"No, there's no reason to be. That beetle is a nice guy. He's a sweet beetle," I told you.

I could hear my own mother's voice in mine as I said these words. Her deep reverence for all creatures had permeated my childhood, always setting me at ease and allowing me a great curiosity toward the animals and insects we encountered together.

"He's a sweet beetle," you repeated. And then we went inside.

For a solid week, Jules, you insisted on checking on this beetle every time we entered or exited the house. It remained there swaying in the breeze, and every day we said hi to it.

"I want to touch it, Mama," you said one morning.

"Sure," I told you. "Touch it. But gently."

Jules, you placed your little fingers beneath it and held them there for a moment. "He's a sweet beetle," you said.

"He really is," I replied.

Vera, you began to touch the beetle every morning as well, and then one morning you asked if we could move him.

"I suppose," I said, again standing there with all of your school stuff in my arms, trying to persuade you to start heading toward the garage. "Where do you want to put him, Vera?"

"Let's put him under the rosebush with the dead butterfly," you suggested.

"Sure," I replied. "That's a nice idea."

So, Vera, you gently scooped him up and carried him reverently in your palm, your little sister tagging along after you, and we all walked over to the rosebush, where you laid him down in the soil.

"Bye, beetle," you said, Vera. And your sister mimicked you. "Bye, beetle."

We got in the car after that and went to school. I picked you up, Jules, at the half-day mark, while you, Vera, stayed at school for the rest of the day, and on our way home, Jules, you told me you wanted to check on the beetle. So we walked over to the rosebush and

## After This

squatted down and there was the dead beetle, still there in the soil.

"He's sad, Mama," you said. "Let's take him in the house."

There was indeed something sad about the beetle lying there in the dry soil under the sun.

"Okay," I said, and I watched as you picked him up so gently and carried him into the house. Jules, you placed him in a little dish on the dining room credenza, and that's exactly where he remains as I write this letter.

I'm writing this little story to you because I know that one day you'll be older and you'll be rushing off somewhere and your arms will be full and you'll be too busy and too caught up to notice a little dead beetle hanging on a spiderweb thread on the stairway.

But you know what? I've loved having that beetle be a part of our lives. I've loved noticing its life and death and its place in our world. There is magic all around us, sweet girls. We just have to remember to embrace it.

Love,

Mama

# Chapter Three

When I sit down with Rabbi Mendel Simons at a Coffee Bean & Tea Leaf in Beverly Hills it's another bright California morning, and Mercedes and BMWs whiz by the busy intersection. Mendel is twenty-eight years old, with pale blue eyes and a ready smile. Originally from Australia, he has a lilting accent and a confidence rare in someone so young.

When I ask him to tell me about his story, he opens up readily. "I'm one of ten siblings. The youngest of us was ten at the time, when my parents were lost in a car accident. They were driving to a wedding from Sydney to Melbourne—I was twenty-five, married, expecting my first child.

"It was a big shock, a devastation to the community in Sydney, Australia. Our parents were so young—fifty-five and forty-nine. I remember being numb a lot. I didn't cry for, like, a year. Well, not after that first week," he says.

I nod, thinking about my own feelings of numbness after my mother died. And this is exactly why I wanted to talk with Rabbi Mendel after meeting him. I find it fascinating that we both lost our parents at such a young age, and that we come from such different backgrounds and cultures.

Judaism has always seemed a little mysterious to me. Although several of my closest friends are Jewish, and I've long been familiar with their customs and holidays, I still don't feel like I know much about the religion itself.

That's why when I met Mendel and his wife and children a month ago, our kids playing together in the airport terminal and then again when we boarded the flight and ended up in the same row of seats, I took a chance and asked his wife, Rachey, if she might know of a rabbi I could speak with.

We were en route from Chicago to Los Angeles and had gotten onto the topic of the hospice I worked for in Chicago, and then onto the research I was doing for this book. Curious about the Jewish perspective on the afterlife, I had hesitantly asked her if she might know a rabbi I could talk to.

Rachey responded with a laugh. "My husband is a rabbi," she said, gesturing across the aisle toward him.

That evening as the plane descended over Los Angeles I stared out the window at the vast city, pondering the kind of fate that had led me to a young rabbi who had also lost his parents. Just this coincidence alone made me wonder about a larger design that I'd perhaps not given enough credence to.

"We moved here to Los Angeles three months later," Mendel says that first day at the coffee shop, about the period following his parents' deaths. "My whole family. Within twelve months I took on marriage, parenthood, losing my parents, moving to Los Angeles, and starting my career."

As I listen to Mendel tell me his story, I'm struck by the differences we share—not just the obvious ones of the sudden death of his parents compared with the long, drawn-out illnesses my parents

## After This

endured, but of the places we were in during those times in our lives. Both of us were parentless and living in Los Angeles at age twenty-five. But where Mendel was married with a child and surrounded by extended family, I was living alone in an apartment by the beach, with no sense of community or faith to guide me through my grief.

I ask him to explain the Judaic view of the afterlife to me.

"Judaism very much focuses on this life," he begins. "Way more than it focuses on the afterlife. In Christianity you ask, where am I going next? In Christianity so much about this life is about where we're going after. Heaven or hell? It's a worry; it's a concern. The Jewish question is more about how have I made this world a better place? It's not about me. It's about the person next to me."

---

I think about what Mendel says about the difference between Christianity and Judaism and flash to a visit I paid to an author named Bill Wiese, who wrote a book called *23 Minutes in Hell*. That summer there were two books floating the *New York Times* bestseller list, *Heaven Is for Real* and *23 Minutes in Hell*, and I read both, fascinated by the conviction with which the writers recount their personal experiences.

In *Heaven Is for Real*, Todd Burpo tells the story of his son, who underwent a near-death experience following an emergency surgery. Often using his son's own words, he explains that four-year-old Colton had an out-of-body experience, during which he was able to see himself being operated on and his family praying for him.

After the surgery Colton Burpo claimed that during his otherworldly experience he met his miscarried sister (whom he had previously known nothing about) as well as his grandfather who died thirty years earlier, sharing details that his family claims he could not have known on his own. Colton also returned from the experience with the message that heaven is for real, Jesus loves children, and that there is a coming battle.

The details of the story are convincing. Colton's near-death experience matches many that have been documented throughout history.

In *23 Minutes in Hell*, author Bill Wiese describes an experience he had one night in his sleep, of being transported to a terrifying place full of fire and violence and demons. He describes the true terror of the isolation he felt during his twenty-three-minute ordeal, just before the hand of God reached down to retrieve him from this torturous place. After regaining consciousness Wiese began to devote his life to researching the scriptures from the Bible that describe hell, and to spreading the message that hell is just as real as the heaven Colton Burpo describes.

In the weeks following my reading of these books I found myself once again struggling to grasp these concepts. All my life various friends and family members have urged me to find God, to accept Jesus Christ into my heart. In times of grief, and in times of strife, multiple people in my life have urged me to seek redemption and comfort through Christianity. In fact, when my first book was published I began to receive occasional e-mails from strangers telling me that I would not be so confused or lost or in pain if I would just open myself up to the teachings of Jesus Christ.

It's not that I've balked at these messages, or even dismissed them altogether. But something in me yet resists them. I believe a large part of my resistance comes from the ways in which religion and politics have become muddled in our culture. A great divide has been created in the past couple of decades, a divide that pits Christianity and right-wing values against liberalism and morality.

It is this divide that has steered me away from a willingness to explore Christian teachings. But I know that just as it is not fair for

## After This

the right wing to dismiss all liberals as lacking in morals, it is not fair for me to fear that accepting the teachings of Jesus Christ means I must become small-minded.

Each time I dismiss concepts of heaven and hell, I worry that I'm wrong. What if they really do exist, and what if everything about how I'm living my life right now dictates that I'm going to one or the other?

The talk I attended by Bill Wiese was given at a church called C3. It's a new church, having been founded by a pastor and his wife, who first began the church in Australia but now held their services in a conference room in the San Diego Marriott. C3 is based on a Pentecostal Christian philosophy that relies on accepting Jesus Christ as one's personal lord and savior. The belief that baptism allows one to live an empowered and fulfilling life plays heavily, as does a belief in spiritual gifts such as divine healing, speaking in tongues, and prophecy.

I took a seat in a folding chair near the back of the conference room and watched as the attendees filed in. The majority of the people were Caucasian, in their thirties and forties. They were dressed casually in the typical California style of jeans, sandals, and flowy tops. I noticed right away that there were a large amount of teenagers present. I watched them with interest. They looked like typical Southern California hipster teens: Chuck Taylors, ripped jeans, logo-strewn T-shirts. They sat in groups, giggling and whispering to each other.

The service opened with a teen rock band. They looked like something you'd see on the Disney Channel, almost a parody of youthful cool. They rocked out, singing in raspy voices about their love of Jesus, and the crowd around me nodded along, tapping their feet and smiling. Memories of my Methodist youth group in Florida came rushing back and I found myself fascinated by these teenagers.

When the band concluded, the minister introduced Bill Wiese.

He is a short, wiry man in his late fifties, and as he took the podium I sat up straighter in my seat for a better view. He began by thanking the church for having him and then took a long, serious look around the room before he began to tell us his story.

For the next fifteen minutes, Wiese told us that he had been a Christian since 1970 but had never studied anything about hell until his experience on November 23, 1998. That night he and his wife went to bed in the top-floor bedroom of their home. It was a regular evening; there was nothing unusual to note about it. Shortly after falling asleep, he said, he was awakened briefly, glanced at the clock and noted the time, and then proceeded to have an out-of-body experience in which he was transported to a small, dark cell. Inside the cell with him were two terrifying creatures.

Bill's voice rose here and he slowed down to describe the horror of these beasts, and the terror he felt. Everyone in the room around me was listening with rapt attention, even the teens. He went on to describe how the beasts threw him against the wall, ripping at his body. He somehow managed to crawl to freedom, only to be confronted by the sound of billions of screaming, tortured souls. He realized then that he was in hell.

Shortly after that Jesus appeared, rescuing him from the misery all around him and explaining that Bill must return to earth and tell everyone he could that hell is real. Wiese awoke, screaming in terror, on the ground floor of his home, in the living room. His first question to his wife, who arrived at his side, was what time it was. He assumed he had been gone for months. It had been twenty-three minutes.

The people around me gasped; some reached for each other in comfort. Bill leaned into the microphone again, urging us to heed his story. He'd made a video, he explained, that further illustrated his message. The lights went down, and for the next twenty minutes we were exposed to a visual reenactment of Wiese's journey to hell. I was enraptured. The video was frightening, like a horror film my parents would have never allowed me to watch when I was a teenager. It was so violent and upsetting that I was in disbelief that we were actually watching it.

In one segment, the story followed two teenagers who were returning home from a party. They had been drinking and the driver was clearly drunk. They crashed on the way home and the teen in the passenger seat died. He was instantly transported to Wiese's version of hell. We saw him in a cell, being ripped apart by monsters, while a voice-over implored his still-living friend to accept Jesus Christ so that he would never have to suffer the same experience. Before he could finish his pleas to his friend, his voice gave way to a tortured scream and then the screen went dark.

When the credits rolled Wiese took the podium again. He looked around the room solemnly. "Hell is real," he said, addressing the audience.

He went on to explain to us that following his experience he returned to earth to study biblical depictions of hell with fervor. The message is simple, he said: If you sin, you go to hell. Any sin, he told us, can land you there—not just the obvious sins, but small ones like lying, stealing a pack of gum, cheating on a test. It was as though he was speaking directly to the teenagers around me. He told us that if any of us had ever done something like this and not repented, not accepted Jesus Christ as our savior, we would surely meet the demise he had described.

When he concluded his sermon he invited audience members to come up to the podium to be "saved." The majority of teenagers in the group stood up, as did a handful of adults. They made their way to the front of the room and stood in a huddle around Wiese. He raised his hands in the air above them, prayed for God to forgive their sins, implored them to bring Jesus into their hearts. The people in the group stood with their heads down, hands clasped. Several of them were crying and shaking. When Wiese finished they turned to hug each other, thanking him profusely, before returning to their seats.

When the whole thing was over I walked outside into the bright California morning. I found myself shaken by Bill's message, by the conviction with which he had spoken, and by the response of the people in the room around me.

I walked off the grounds of the Marriott until I could see the ocean, and I leaned against a railing, looking out at the great, wide Pacific. I thought about Julie, about my parents. If hell is real, and if what Bill Wiese says is true about how we end up there, then my parents and my friend are currently being ripped apart by demons. For that matter, all those kids—all those people—who died in that flood in Pakistan recently are there too.

The message was a fearful one. Terrifying, in fact. I thought about all those teenagers in the conference room. I wondered about the paths they were embarking on, if they would stay with the church or not, and where their lives would lead them. I thought about myself as a teenager, about all the ways I had rebelled, about all the horrible behavior that had resulted from my losses, and about the times I'd lied or cheated, or hurt people out of my own sense of suffering and pain.

I've repented for those actions in my own way; I have sought to understand and forgive myself. I've done my best to atone for my actions, trying to lead a good and purposeful life in the years since. But I have failed to develop a belief system that involves Jesus Christ. If Bill Wiese's hell is real, then I am going there too.

I'm thinking about all this during my meeting with Rabbi Mendel, who reiterates his statement. "Judaism very much focuses on this life,"

## After This

he says again. "Why focus on the afterlife? Because if it's all about the person next to you, not about you, then what matters after the person dies is what they have done, the legacy they have left behind, and how that affects the world. And so Judaism focuses on how the people who died are very much still alive in this world through what they have left behind."

I feel an immediate sense of relief, the relief of not focusing on the afterlife, when he says this. And I think about my parents—who they were, the things they did in their lives, the actions they took, the things they taught me.

Mendel continues, "I remember standing in my dad's bedroom and looking at his clothing three days after he died. Nobody remembers him for the car he drove or the shirts he wore. People remember him for the stories he left behind with the people coming by to pay respects. The guy who was going to get evicted, but my dad stepped in to help him out. People remember him for the smiles, for uplifting their days. People remember him for the impact he had on other people's lives, what he was able to do for other people. If he was able to influence other people, then that is what he left behind."

The word *afterlife* begins to take on new meaning as I listen to Mendel. I've never thought that much about the afterlife being part of *this* life. But he's right. My parents have continued to live on in many ways—not just through me, but through the things they created during their lives, the relationships they had with people, and the generosity and good deeds they bestowed on others.

"But that still can't be everything," I say. "We're always going to be curious about where we're going next, right?"

"Sure, of course. To a certain extent. In the Jewish afterlife there is a whole world of where the soul goes afterwards," Mendel explains. "The soul rests and goes through a cleansing process, and ultimately ends up in the Garden of Eden, commonly known as heaven. But the main thing is that the soul is put down in this world to elevate, to bring about a fusion between the physical and the spiritual. We perceive godliness as something removed from the physical. People often say, 'Right now I'm too busy making a living. In a few years when I've made my pile of cash, then I'll have time to be spiritual.' But the truth is, being spiritual is right here, right now in your material existence. Being honest in all your dealings. Being a good husband, parent, employer, employee."

I like thinking about a blend of spirituality and reality, I realize. One of the things I struggle with most when it comes to the afterlife is when a particular belief separates the two in an extreme fashion. Maybe that's why I'm drawn to visiting mediums. I yearn for a way to incorporate this world with the next. I tell Mendel about some of my visits to the psychics.

He nods. "I struggle with that," he says. "Everyone is always saying things like, 'Grandma and Grandpa are smiling down at us at this wedding. They're proud of you.' I could never relate. I've always felt like it's just a therapeutic way of making us feel good. It's our human way of making ourselves feel better. They're not proud of me. They're not here anymore. They *would* have been proud of me is a better way to say it, I think.

"On the other hand," Mendel continues, "there's a spiritual way of being able to wrap our human minds around things. When someone dies they're not physical anymore. But this physical world is mirrored by the spiritual realm. This spiritual world is like the back end of a website—the physical world is what you see on the screen."

I flash back to my question to psychic medium John Edward, when I asked him where the deceased are. "Where is the Internet?" he asked rhetorically. "You can't see it, but it's there; it's affecting everything all the time." I realize that at this point in my journey, I'm more open than ever to believing in something bigger than I can perceive. Yet I still can't shake my anxiety about death.

"I'm so afraid that I'm going to die and leave my own daughters," I tell Mendel. "I have this constant uneasiness, not necessarily about where I'm going next, but more about what will happen when I'm gone."

He nods at me. "I've never had those fears," he says. "When my parents died everyone else had those fears. I think it has a lot to do with deeply understanding and internalizing the concept that it's not in your hands."

"Easier said than done," I reply.

"I know, I know," he says, smiling. "It's easy for me to say, but how easy is it to feel? We live in a world where there is a divine plan. Our time is given to us by God. At the end of the day it's not in our hands. Are you going to get that job? Crack that deal? Beat that disease? It's not in your hands."

I admire his conviction. I envy it. I wish I believed wholeheartedly that there is indeed a divine plan. That my parents' deaths were part of it. That Julie's death was part of it.

"But it's more complex than that," Mendel continues. "We still have to do the best job we can. Even though there is a divine plan, we have everything to do with how it all turns out. Meaning, it's very different in the Christian perspective. In Christianity it's all about your feelings, your intention. In Judaism we care that you believe in God, but we don't care as much about your feelings or intentions. The bottom line is action."

I find some relief in hearing these things. He's right, I think. There is nothing I can do. I'm constantly explaining to my clients that anxiety and obsessive worry are simply a way of making yourself feel like you're doing something, when really, you're just wasting energy on something you have no control over. But again, I realize this is easier said than done, especially when I struggle to put it into practice myself.

Mendel looks at me. "Your job in this world is to be the best person, best mom, best writer you can be. Your job is to not worry about what's going to happen later. Your job is to worry about how much of an asset you are now."

I nod at him. There really is nothing I can do besides the things he's telling me. There is nothing I can do for my children that I'm not doing. Worrying about what will happen if I die and leave them will not make anything better.

I nod at him some more, mulling these things over, and we begin to talk about the idea of being of service. I tell him how after my father died I slumped into a deep depression for almost a year. I didn't work; I tried to write a book, but I couldn't find the words. I spent most of those months on the couch, crying and wondering what the point of my existence was.

Strangely enough, it was another young man, a writer named Dave Eggers, who became responsible for my emergence from that depression. I had been drawn to Eggers after his 1999 memoir, A Heartbreaking Work of Staggering Genius, in which he documented the loss of both of his parents by the time he was twenty-two, and his struggles to care for his younger brother in the wake of those losses. At the time I had never encountered someone my age who had been through anything similar, and I followed Eggers's work with interest. A year after my father died, Dave Eggers opened a branch of his nonprofit tutoring center, 826LA, down the street from me and I began volunteering there.

I tell Mendel about all this, explaining to him that my parents never really taught me the art of being of service to others. They were kind and generous people, but they were not people who volunteered regularly or instilled that drive in me. But suddenly there I was at this tutoring center every day, spending my afternoons helping underprivileged schoolkids with their homework. One day a few months into it, I was walking home and I realized that for the first time in a long time I felt good again. My life didn't seem so meaningless. I wasn't dwelling on my sadness so much anymore. I had purpose, and I woke up every day excited to work with those kids again.

"Exactly," Mendel says in response. "Happiness is a by-product of living a meaningful and purposeful life. Anyone who is living a life that is larger than materialism, a life that has higher purpose . . . Well, the by-product of that is almost always happiness. You don't have to pursue happiness; you just need to live a purposeful life, a meaningful life. Whenever I'm feeling down or unmotivated in my life the first thing I'll do is go and do someone a favor. Lift someone up, help somebody. Nothing gives me more energy and drive than that."

"Yes," I agree. "People ask me all the time if I get drained from the work I do, but it's the opposite. I'll go into a day at my office feeling tired or weighed down by my life, and then I'll see several clients and come out feeling more energized and peaceful than I did going in."

I think about how some of my most inspiring sessions have been working with clients of different cultural backgrounds or religious affinities. In grad school it seemed intimidating to work with someone who was very different from me, but in fact I've found that some of the most interesting work arises from these relationships. I believe that good therapy means helping someone explore their own beliefs and constructs. So often I've found that when I'm coming from a place of not knowing I can ask simple questions that I myself am curious about, which lead to clients having to explain their beliefs in a way they may not have done in a while.

Mendel tells me about the organization, Young Jewish Professionals, that he started when he moved to Los Angeles several years ago. He explains that it's a way of creating and sustaining a sense of community for Jewish people in their twenties and thirties who are focused on their careers but who perhaps live far away from their families, or who have not yet created families. We discuss how this is a huge shift in our culture from forty to fifty years ago. And again, I think about the lack of support and community I had in my life when I lost my parents.

"It has a big impact on the grief process," I tell him. "The community, or lack of it, around you." And he agrees readily, pausing for a moment to reflect again on our different experiences.

I ask him what advice he would give to someone who yearns to still feel connected to his or her lost loved ones, and he returns to the notion of action.

"Again, my dad didn't take anything with him—his car, his clothes," he explains. "But people kept coming to the house and telling us about these gifts. One guy said he loaned him money. One guy said he helped him out when he was sick. That's what stayed here. All the acts of kindness my parents did in this world. Everything they stood for, the children they raised, the values they imparted in those children. That stays here and now we're continuing to develop what they started.

"A favor you did for someone, the light you spread," he goes on, "that never goes away. So people who die . . . they now live through us."

He continues, "Judaism talks about the afterlife, how the soul goes through these elevation stations until it gets to heaven. Here on earth we try to elevate their souls by doing what's called a mitzvah. It's when you go out and do some act of kindness in someone's name. When you do this it elevates their soul. When I do something my parents taught me to do, I'm connecting with them in those moments. They're with me in those moments. That drives me. It gives me purpose, and it gives me a relationship with them."

On my way home from my last meeting with Mendel, all I can think about are the times I've wondered if my parents could see me. Could they see me at my college graduation, or whenever I accomplished something I was really proud of, or when I gave birth to my daughters?

I realize that it doesn't really matter if they can see me. What matters is that I did something that they *would have been* proud of, something that carries forth the values they taught me and the goodness they stood for. That's what matters.

One night I come across an old nightgown that belonged to me as a girl.

"Vera," I say, holding up the garment, "I used to wear this to bed when I was a little girl."

The nightgown has a series of pastel satin heart-shaped balloons across the front. She puts it on immediately, admiring herself in the mirror.

"Is this what you looked like when you wore it, Mommy?" she asks, turning to model it for me.

I nod, a smile on my face.

"Who gave this to you?" she asks, running her fingers over the satin balloons.

"My mom did."

"And then she died?"

"Well, she died later, when I was a bit older."

"How did she die?"

I find Vera's questions about death refreshing. In our culture, when we learn of a death in someone's life, it is disrespectful to come right out and ask *how*, even though that is often the first question on our minds.

I have told Vera many times how my own mother died, but I answer her question again patiently. "She got really, really sick. She had a disease called cancer. And one day her body just got so tired that it didn't work anymore and she died."

"No, but, like, *how* did she die?" Vera throws herself back on the bed and flings her arms out to her sides. She twists her head to one side and closes her eyes. "Like this? Did it look like this?"

I'm constantly amazed by the way she sees the world, breaking it down into such simple ideas, making me realize just how complex and nuanced adult concepts can be.

"Yes, I guess it was kind of like that." I can't help but laugh a little, looking at her little form splayed out this way.

Vera sits up, looking satisfied. "Was she in a bed?"

"Yes, a hospital bed." I wait for her to ask what happened to the body, but she doesn't. I'm relieved. I'm not sure I'm ready to explain the concept of cremation to a four-year-old.

"And then your dad died?" she asks next.

"Well, he died about seven years later."

"How old were you, Mama?"

"I was twenty-five when my father died," I reply, knowing as I say it that it will be impossible for her to comprehend that age.

"And how old were you when your mom died?"

"I was eighteen."

"Is that grown-up or little?"

"Well, it's not quite grown-up, but not little either. Either way it was too soon for someone to lose their mom," I tell her. Tears well up in my eyes at this point.

## After This

Vera pats me on my knee then, and says the thing she always says when I get sad about my parents. "It's okay, Mama. You have me now."

There's something incredible to me about this statement. It's such a simple one, but also such an intuitive one. She's right. Becoming a mother really did make my parents' deaths okay. Having a daughter has made it easier not to have a mother.

I am thinking about this when Vera poses her next question: "Where are they?"

"My parents?"

This is the first time she has actually asked *where* they are. Up until now she has just taken it at face value that they are "gone."

I open my mouth to answer, and then close it again. I am not sure what I want to tell her. Do I want to introduce her to the idea of heaven? It seems like such a comforting image for a child to process, but I feel uncomfortable offering up this concept when I don't believe in it myself.

That night I decide to just be honest. I put my arms around her. "Honey, I don't know where they are. No one really knows what happens when people die. Some people think they know, they believe certain things, but really no one knows for sure."

Vera continues to trace the satin hearts on her nightgown with her fingertip. "Okay, Mama," she says simply.

I lean my cheek against the top of her head and I think about the messages from Bill Wiese and Rabbi Mendel. "The important thing is that we live good lives while we are here. That we honor the world we are part of and that we continue to live lives that your grandparents would be proud of. The important thing is that we leave this world a better place than it was when we found it."

"How do we do that, Mama?" she asks.

"Well, sweetie, in lots of ways. We help others who aren't as fortunate as us. We are kind to everyone we encounter. We create art and beauty and honor pain and sadness. We act with intention. . . ." I trail off, remembering that I am talking to a four-year-old.

I look at Vera. She's still tracing the lines of the hearts on her nightgown. I know she may not understand all of this now, but I also know that the best way for her to learn these concepts is to see them in action through the people around her. I know that when I die I want to feel that she will continue to embody the principles I have learned to care about in my lifetime. And I know that she will.

That night, going to sleep, I feel a little less afraid of what it would be like if something happened to me. I know that life would continue. That my daughters would continue, all of us perpetuating a beautiful cycle of human existence.

# After This

Dear Vera and Jules,

One of the things I most wish to impart to you is a sense of privilege. I'm writing this letter from the patio of our home in Santa Monica. Jules, you are taking a nap, and Vera, you are still at your little preschool down the road. It's a Wednesday afternoon and the warm California breeze washes past me, and I'm so glad that we have this beautiful life together.

But it's often moments like this when I most want you to be aware of what a privilege it is to live this way. We are not well off by any means. I rent the house we live in and often struggle to contend with the high cost of living that comes with dwelling in this part of the world, yet we live a comfortable life in a safe place.

You will likely go on to earn bachelor's and even master's degrees. You have a future that will probably involve obtaining jobs that you enjoy and that earn a decent income. You will travel to beautiful places and you will eat lavish meals. You will buy pretty clothes and you will indulge in all sorts of things that come your way. You will find yourself surrounded by peers who are experiencing similar lifestyles and you will probably spend a large portion of your childhood and adolescence not questioning this way of life.

I struggle with this, though. On the one hand I want you to have everything you could ever want. I want you to have everything I listed above, and more. But I only want those things for you if you are able to appreciate what a great gift they are, and only if you can remain aware that not everyone in the world lives this way, only if you can make a point in your life to give of yourself to people who need more.

Last month for your fifth birthday, Vera, we went to the American Girl store with your best friend and her mother. We let you girls each pick out a doll that resembled you and then we all sat down to lunch in their café. The dolls you chose had their own seats and were even given little plates and cups. You and your friend were utterly delighted and her mom and I sipped mimosas and watched you revel in the experience.

I was happy for you. It was quite a magical thing for you to take your dolls out to lunch like that, but I felt troubled by it all as well. I adore you, my sweet girl, and all I want is to give you a million fun and lavish gifts, but I want so much for you to be aware of how special it is that you get to have things like this.

As you both grow older I want to impart a sense of meaning into everything we do. I want to teach you how to give back to the world around you, even more than you receive. I don't want to take the same expensive vacations my parents took, to beautiful locales where we basked at resorts. Instead I want to travel to places where you can gain a broader sense of the world at large, and perhaps do work that will benefit the world in some way.

If for some reason I'm not here when you're older to do these things with you, I want you to promise me that you'll always find a way to be of service to the world. There is a difference between helping and serving. Helping implies that you are above something, that

## After This

something is broken. But serving implies that you are giving of yourself to something that is equally valuable in its existence.

You are not better than anyone you encounter, but you do have more privileges than a lot of the people you will meet in this world. Serve the world and you will serve yourself. Give of yourself and you will receive in return.

It took me a long time to find my way to a path of service. I worked at fancy magazines and I traveled on their dime. I reviewed restaurants and spent inordinate amounts of time thinking about the nuances of gourmet cuisine. And then I came home and wondered why my life felt meaningless. These things were fun and glamorous, but they were empty.

It was when I found ways to give of myself, when I found ways to attempt to make the world a better place, that my life began to feel meaningful and fulfilling. This is a simple truth, but one that we so often forget.

Do more with yourselves. Do more with all that you have been given. Build things, build ideas, build better places, serve others who are struggling to make their way alongside you. Use your one wild and precious life to make this world a better place.

Promise me that you will do this, and I promise you that you will never feel empty.

With love,

*Mama*

## Chapter Four

My vision is clouded initially, and then, like a camera lens pulling back, everything suddenly comes into focus: an old-fashioned wood-burning stove, a heavy, cast-iron teakettle with steam that is just beginning to thread upward from the spout. I am a woman in my thirties, standing before this stove, immobile with sadness.

The steam grows thicker and pours forth in a plume of ghostly white, but I make no move to grasp the kettle or turn down the heat. I am filled with a deep sorrow that makes my limbs feel heavy and paralyzed.

"What do you see?" a soft male voice asks close to my ear.

My own voice seems to come from another place. It is thick and slow, unrecognizable, as though I have been sedated. I have been, I suppose.

"An old stove, a teakettle," I answer.

"Where are you?" the voice prompts again.

"In my kitchen at home," I mumble. It is here in the vision when I finally turn away from the stove and notice the room around me. It is a simple room, with wood walls and a bare floor. A window looks out on a prairie, fields spreading out into the distance.

"How do you feel?" asks the voice.

"I feel sad. So sad."

"Yes, good. Let yourself feel that. Why are you sad?"

"I don't know," I say, and in the vision I leave the kitchen, walking past an entryway with a staircase that leads up to the second floor, and then into a parlor decorated with a simple sofa and chairs. A gas lantern sits on the mantel above the fireplace.

I stop in my tracks just after crossing the threshold of the room. On the sofa lies the body of a small boy. "Ohhh," I say in my slurred voice.

"Yes, what is it?" asks the voice.

"A boy. My son. He is dead."

"Yes, I understand. Tell me more," the voice says.

But I don't want to tell him more. I am overcome with grief. My son is dead. My beautiful little boy. Tears begin to slide down my cheeks.

"Yes, yes, that's it," says the man's voice, and then I feel him gently blotting at my tears with a tissue.

I am suddenly in two places at once.

In reality I am in Sedona, Arizona, lying on my back in the home office of Michael C. Brown, a licensed psychotherapist specializing in past-life regression. But in my head I am standing in this dusty parlor, in who knows what decade, grieving the loss of a child. The emotions I feel are incredibly real, the grief inside me opening up like a chasm.

But the feeling of Kleenex on my face also feels real, as does Michael's overly soothing voice so close to my head. I can sense myself coming out of the vision and back into the office, but as Michael instructed me prior to the session, I try to let go of the rational thoughts that are working so hard to persuade me that this is total bullshit, and I return to the woman in the parlor.

# After This

The drive to Sedona, Arizona, was a seven-hour straight shot east from Los Angeles. I brought along with me my friend Denise, a woman I've known for close to two years, someone who shares my experience of grief. Denise lost her husband to a sudden heart attack a few years ago, when she was only thirty-seven.

On the drive to Sedona we spoke at length about the lingering effects of grief. We both agreed that even after the immediate loss—the days of crying, the nights of insomnia, the feelings of isolation and loneliness—subsides, there is still the lingering curiosity about what all this means. Losing someone you love throws your whole life into question. What are we doing here? What is the point of all this? Why do some people die young or in horrific accidents or awful illnesses, and others live until they are ninety?

These questions become louder and louder following a loss. They come in waves, and in the kind of stages that Elisabeth Kübler-Ross writes about. The grieving person's mind turns these questions over and over, worrying them like a stone, rearranging them like a Rubik's Cube. *Why did they have to go? Where did they go? Is there something I can do to bring them back? Will I ever see them again?*

Eventually the thoughts grow quieter. They are part of the grieving process. After a while they go from a loud staccato to a low hum in the back of your head as life once again resumes its course, but they never disappear completely. When you lose someone you love, your whole existence can be thrown into question. But for those who have not lost someone significant these questions may never arise. When you haven't experienced grief, life can seem predictable and reliable; there can be no real need to wonder why. But for those of us who have, the questions abound.

On the drive to Sedona it was all Denise and I could talk about.

I'd decided to explore the realm of past-life regression as part of my search for answers, and I was on my way to do a session with Michael C. Brown, a psychotherapist well known for his work in helping clients explore their previous lives.

I felt like I was pushing boundaries in my grief work at that point. Past-life regression seemed like the edge of some new-agey realm, but I rationalized it by thinking about how past-life guru Brian Weiss was once a traditional therapist and was swayed into this work by the healing experiences he had with his clients. I already knew that even if I didn't believe that the visions and experiences people have when regressed are actually real, I think there is therapeutic value to analyzing them as one would a dream.

Sedona is a mecca of new age mysticism. Nestled about two hours north of Phoenix, the small city is characterized by its enormous red rock formations, and the Native American presence dates as far back as 9000 BC. The land is rich in history and a sense of reverence. It's also touristy. Brightly colored pink jeeps are parked by the dozen along the main street, promising tourists mind-blowing trips out into the red rocks. New age shops line the sidewalks, giant crystal displays glittering in the windows, and there are more spas than I could hope to visit in a month.

We checked into our hotel and loosely unpacked our things. That morning, before leaving Los Angeles, I'd taken a pregnancy test. There was a very small chance that I might be due with my second child, but the test had been negative. I felt a moment of relief when I saw the test result, still not sure if I was ready to expand our little family, and I had happily thrown a box of tampons in my suitcase.

That night at dinner Denise and I chatted about the next day's schedule. My session with Michael Brown was scheduled for the next morning, and then Denise and I planned to do some exploring. I found myself trying to articulate to her why I'm interested in past lives, and as I did so, I realized just how comfortable our culture has become with the concept of reincarnation. Notions of karma and multiple lives are tossed about in pop culture as though our major religions rely upon them. But the thing is that Christianity, the most popular religion in this country, does not actually embrace these concepts.

"But how often do you hear someone say something like, 'Oh, you must have been a chef in your past life'?" I asked Denise. "Or how often do you hear someone blame a car accident or a breakup on karma, without even really understanding the deeper spiritual implications of just such a phrase?"

Even though these concepts date as far back as some of the most ancient Eastern religions, they have now permeated everything from modern-day song lyrics to Facebook status updates.

Living in Los Angeles, a bastion of new age spirituality and self-help, I've been hearing stories about people doing past-life regressions for as long as I've been here. Friends have told me fantastical tales about uncovering past lives and claimed that the experiences have helped them understand exactly what they're going through here in this lifetime. I've always been extremely skeptical. Truthfully, past-life regression seems ridiculous to me. But again, that curiosity in me abounds. What if it's really true?

I have to admit that I find the idea comforting. The concept of living multiple lives means that we never really die. We simply migrate into a new existence. It means that the people we lose don't ever really die either, and that we might in fact encounter them again, either here in this very life or in another. And even though I don't really believe it, I would love to think that my father has metamorphosed into one of his beloved hummingbirds, or that my mother is living out a whole new life in a body that is free of illness.

As I delve into my research, I try to have an open mind. Reincarnation is simply the idea that the soul or spirit begins a new life after a person's physical death. Depending on the philosophy, this new life could take the form of another human, animal, or even spiritual self. This belief permeates hundreds of different religions and philosophies, most of them adhering to the notion that each lifetime comprises a certain number of "lessons" that are learned until a soul reaches enlightenment.

I think about how many times people have commented on someone I know being an "old soul" or a "young one." In fact, my own mother, baffled by my constant insistence on contemplating my existence, used to tell me that I was an old soul. "You're so much wiser than I ever was," she told me once when I was in high school. I scoffed at her at the time, but now as I read about reincarnation I try to fit this memory into the frame. What if I *have* been around for centuries? What if I was my mother's mother in another lifetime?

This is about the time when my rational mind takes over, arguing that the concept of reincarnation is a crutch, something dreamed up so that we do not have to face the raw pain of absence. It's a way of softening the blow of loss. I acknowledge this argument, but continue pushing through with my research. I am fascinated by the stories I keep reading. Tales of children who remember their previous lives, which upon investigation turn out to be based on the life of an actual person, such as a war soldier, whom they could have otherwise known nothing about.

One of the most popular books on the subject, *Many Lives, Many Masters*, was written by the aforementioned Dr. Brian Weiss, an American psychotherapist who, after a series of uncanny experiences with one of his patients, was driven to explore the notion of past lives, and has since devoted his life's work to the subject. While Weiss is notoriously hard to get a session with, I found a list of recommended therapists specializing in regression on his website, which is how I came to find myself in Sedona in the office of Michael C. Brown.

## After This

Originally a traditional psychotherapist with a master's degree in clinical social work, Brown claims he was drawn to past-life regression after a series of "paranormal" events in his life that led him to believe there is a deeper meaning to our lives than most people give credit to. In an explanation on his website, Brown explains past-life regression in this manner:

> Most of us have lived many other lives... same soul, many bodies, as Dr. Weiss would say. Past life regression therapy is a therapeutic modality by which it is possible to retrieve memories our soul has of lives it has lived before. The soul possesses a kind of cellular memory, and can remember every experience it has ever had in any body, in all of our previous lives. Remembering these lives and important experiences and relationships within them can often reveal the root cause of a number of different kinds of problems. These problems can be carried over into this life we are living now. Lifelong illnesses and specific symptoms such as chronic pain, unexplainable fears and phobias, depression, severe anxiety, panic attacks, repeating destructive relationships, etc., often have their beginnings in another life. Past Life Regression Therapy provides an opportunity to see and remember when these symptoms first began. As we become aware of how, when and where the issue first began, our understanding can result in growth and amazing changes. Significant reduction or complete elimination of symptoms and problems is common. This is often true, whether the problem is emotional, spiritual, physical... or all three.

I booked my appointment with an open mind, reminding myself that there was absolutely no point in doing this if I couldn't at least attempt to open up to the experience. I had never been hypnotized, which is the method used leading into the regression, and I felt the most nervous about this. Who knew what might come forth if someone were able to really get me into that state?

---

Michael Brown operates out of his home, perched up on a hill, overlooking the red rock canyons. In a series of e-mails that we exchanged while arranging the visit, he explained to me that our session would last anywhere from three to five hours. He would begin by talking with me for a while about how regression works, then exploring my current life issues, and what has led me to seek an understanding about my past lives. After that the regression would take place in his home office.

Michael greets me at the front door. He is in his fifties and looks a little like the actor Michael Caine. He is brusque and businesslike as he ushers me into his home, directing me to a set of chairs by a window, but he warms up considerably as we begin to talk. I tell him that I have worked in hospice and experienced a series of significant losses in my life. I explain a little about the book I'm working on, and he lights up, excited to talk about his craft.

For the next forty-five minutes Michael recounts a series of paranormal experiences he had in his life that led him to pursue this work. From a story about his dead grandmother appearing before him when he was a child, to seeing a UFO outside his boyhood home, to a set of out-of-body experiences during college, he explains that he is a firm believer in the spiritual realm. He seems to enjoy talking about his experiences, and after a while, I begin to feel like the counselor, with Michael as my client. He even becomes emotional at one point, and sings an a cappella version of the Beatles song "Blackbird." He grips his UFO mug of tea tightly while he sings with his eyes closed; my stomach tightens, wondering what, exactly, I've gotten myself into.

## After This

Finally we head to Michael's office, where he instructs me to lie back on a queen-size bed after removing my shoes. Again, a feeling of anxiety hits me. *What am I doing?* I ask myself, as he arranges several blankets over me, explaining that patients often become chilled during the regression. He sets up a chair next to my head and places an eye pillow over my forehead and eyes. I take a few deep breaths and try to center myself as Michael begins the regression, reminding myself that there is no point in doing this if I'm not at least willing to give it a real shot.

He starts by leading me through a simple technique to relax my body, asking me to concentrate on letting go of tension throughout my limbs. Then he instructs me to envision a staircase leading down into a beautiful garden, encouraging me to walk through the garden admiring the flowers and plants around me. Exercises like this don't come easy for me. It is difficult to turn off the endless stream of thoughts that flow through my brain, to turn off my critical, skeptical mind and really let the visions unfold, but I try my best.

Michael asks me to notice the sky above me and to let myself float upward into one of the clouds. His voice is slow and calm, but it's saturated with a sticky sweetness that makes me feel as though he is talking to a child. However, I do as he instructs, and picture myself floating serenely up into the clouds. His voice is there, reminding me that I am deeply relaxed, that I am open to the experience of whatever comes next.

"Okay," he says next. "When you come down from the cloud you will be in a lifetime that is of great significance to your soul. Begin to descend now."

I feel myself take a deep breath as I release from the cloud, floating down. My vision is blurred at first, and then the kitchen in the house on the prairie swims into focus.

Later, looking back, I will have to admit that the kitchen, the teakettle, the old stove, and the feeling of immense grief are a profound experience. All of it looks and feels decidedly different from the rest of the images of the garden and the clouds and the staircase. There is a sharp clarity to it, and the emotions that come are intense. Standing in that parlor, looking down at the little boy's body laid out on the sofa, feels beyond something I could cultivate in my imagination. The vision is crisp and overwhelming.

But as the regression continues the sharpness fades. I find myself conjuring the images in a way that feels similar to when I write fiction, the times when I let myself space out while driving or showering, picturing the lives of my characters and letting the ideas just flow forth.

I do not like having to speak aloud to Michael. The sound of my own voice, and then of his, distracts me and pulls me out of the visions. After grieving the boy, I tell him that the woman in my vision goes upstairs to pack a bag.

"There is nothing more for me here now," I tell Michael. "And my father is coming, so I have to leave. He is not a good man." Again, this feels like a construction of my imagination, but I just keep talking. I go on to tell Michael that my father is a violent man and now that my son is dead I intend to leave this town for good. As I speak I have to tell myself to stop thinking about how this sounds like a bad Lifetime movie.

Michael continues to murmur in my ear. "Yes, good," he says. "Spirit, please guide Claire to the next most important event in this woman's life."

He is quiet for a few minutes and I just float there in my imagination until he speaks again. "What is happening now?" he asks.

In the next vision, I am on a stage as the lead singer in an opera. It is years past the death of my son and I have gone on to become a famous singer who travels the world. I find myself cringing as I recite these details aloud to Michael. The idea of singing on a stage is probably my

## After This

worst nightmare (along with dancing), not to mention that the notion of fame and success in a past life seems utterly hackneyed.

Michael prods me with questions, attempting to guide me deeper into this woman's life. He asks me about the time period and I tell him it's the 1950s. He asks me how I feel and I tell him that I am still lonely and sad, despite my success. I answer each question he asks with the first thing that comes to my mind, again as though I am dreaming up the details of a character for a novel.

I'm not sure how much time has passed at this point, but I am becoming more and more aware of the room around me. My body has become stiff and uncomfortable and I just want to be done with this whole thing. I consider sitting up and just telling Michael that I am finished, but for some reason, I do not want to disappoint him. He seems so genuinely invested in my visions.

When he asks again for the spirit to guide me to the next significant moment in this woman's life, I outright lie to him, desperate to bring an end to this session.

When Michael asks where I am next I reply, "I'm in a hospital bed. I'm very old."

"Yes, yes, good," he says. "You appear to be at the end of this lifetime. Is anyone there with you?"

"No," I mumble. "I'm all alone." Great, I think to myself. I'm lying to a past-life regressionist. Surely *this* is bad karma. I almost laugh out loud.

"Yes, yes," he says. "You have to come to the end. It is time to release your soul from this woman and go back to the spirit realm. Feel yourself detaching and floating back up into the clouds."

I let myself envision the clouds, finally relaxing again now that I know we're almost done.

"You are spirit once more. You are at peace. Ask yourself now, what was the lesson of this lifetime?"

I struggle to come up with an answer. I mumble something about grief and how even though I went on to become successful, I was never able to enjoy it because I spent my life consumed by grief.

"Yes, yes, good," Michael says, and then he leads me back through the garden and up the staircase, before finally removing my eye pillow and helping me to sit up.

He automatically hands me a glass of water, and asks how I feel.

"Okay, I guess. I feel cold, and a little dizzy," I reply truthfully.

"Do you want to know how long the regression was?" he asks.

"Sure," I say.

"Almost two hours."

"Wow." I am genuinely shocked and I glance at the clock to verify that he is correct. He is.

Before I leave Michael hands me a USB drive containing an audio recording of our session. He tells me to take care of myself in the coming days, and cautions me that I may feel waves of emotion following today's session. He reminds me that he is available at any point to talk and offers to do some processing of the session right here, but I tell him that I'd rather do so on my own, and thank him for everything, eager to leave.

On the drive back to the hotel to meet Denise, I replay the experience in my head. I have decidedly mixed feelings. On the one hand, it all seems utterly ridiculous. I do not feel as though I have just visited a past lifetime. Yet, at the same time, I am strangely appreciative of the experience, if only as an exercise. I find inherent value in the products of our imagination, viewing them as a resource for examining feelings that may exist in an unconscious realm.

If I view the regression as a dream I would analyze, then I can see very much how the lifetime of this young grieving mother relates to my own experience in my current life. The grieving mother allows me to reverse my own experience of losing a mother, to imagine it as a

## After This

mirror image. Also, that the woman found success yet still was unable to quell her grief is indicative of how I have written a memoir about my parents' deaths yet continue to feel the pain of that loss.

The only piece of the regression that nags me is the initial vision of standing before that stove. The picture was so clear, and it was unlike anything I have ever experienced. I have never seen a stove like the one in my vision, and while most of the regression felt like something I was conjuring up from my imagination, the initial scene was one that felt like it came from elsewhere.

The day after I return from Sedona I realize that my period is now four days late. I take another test, and this time it is positive. In the bathroom I stand before the mirror and lay my hands on my belly. There is a new person growing inside me. Everything about this fact seems strange considering my recent experiences. What if this baby is someone I have experienced other lifetimes with? What are the lessons he is coming here to learn? What lifetime is she leaving behind?

I shake my head at myself in the mirror, wondering if all this stuff is beginning to make me a little crazy.

---

The following month I take a seat in the home office of Gahl Sasson. Gahl is a well-known astrologer, based in Los Angeles, and he has come highly recommended as a past-life regressionist. Unlike Michael Brown, Gahl uses the ancient Jewish sect of Kabbalah as well as astrology in his practice, linking our current and past lives to our astrological charts.

"We make contracts before entering each new lifetime," he explains. "We decide which lessons we are here to learn, and we reincarnate with other souls who are specifically here to help us experience those lessons."

"So basically you're saying that I contracted with my parents before I was even born that I would come here and be their daughter and that they would die?" I ask blatantly.

"In essence, yes," Gahl replies. "Losing them, and even them dying, were experiences that all three of you needed to have in order to fulfill your soul's evolution."

I frown. Part of me wants to blindly accept this. What a fantastically concrete answer to the one question that has run through my head a thousand times in the past decade. *Why did my parents have to die?*

Before I can ask any more questions Gahl begins to analyze my astrological chart.

"Birth date, time, and place," Gahl commands, before I've even gotten comfortable in my chair. In his midforties, he is originally from Israel, and my nicety so far has had little effect on his brusque manner.

"Uh, May 21, 1978; 2:48 p.m.; Atlanta, Georgia," I tell him.

Gahl proceeds to say a lot of things about my moons and Saturns and Uranuses, my rising sign in conjunction with whatnot, but then quickly gets to the heart of it.

"You're supposed to be doing two things in this life," he says, and I perk up.

"Writing and communication. It shows here that you should be writing books, publishing articles, essays, giving talks, teaching."

I nod. "And the second thing?"

"You have Mercury in Scorpio. Mercury is the planet of communication and writing. Your moon is in Scorpio, the house of death. That means you need to be working with death, writing about death. Have you heard the term *psychopomp*?"

I shake my head. I haven't.

"A psychopomp is someone who bridges this life to the afterlife, for others. So in essence, what these two things are saying is that you need to be writing about death, communicating about death, helping people to understand death."

I am speechless. I am here, in Gahl's office, specifically for the purpose of writing this book about the afterlife, something he could not possibly have known. "And you can see all this in my chart?" I ask.

"Yes," he replies perfunctorily.

We talk for a while then. He gives me some important dates in the year ahead, explains more nuances of my chart to me, and tells me to expect a great expansion of some sort around June 15 of the following year. The new baby I am carrying is due June 17. I am not obviously pregnant, only nine weeks along at this point, but when I tell him this he nods as if it all makes perfect sense to him.

Then we move on to the real reason I have come, which is to attempt another past-life regression.

It's been only a month since my session with Michael in Sedona, and I'm still kind of cringing over the whole thing. It seemed so fabricated to me that I'm honestly not looking forward to trying it again. However, I have to admit that I find Gahl's businesslike manner about the whole thing refreshing in comparison to Michael Brown's cloying and overly invested manner.

Gahl comes around from behind his desk, reclines the chair I am seated in, places a blanket over my torso and a mask over my eyes, and begins to lead me through a very similar meditation to the one Michael Brown took me through. Again, I descend a great staircase into a beautiful garden, and then up into the clouds. When it is time for me to step into the past life, I immediately feel myself block up.

"What do you see?" Gahl asks.

"Nothing," I stammer.

"Start small," he says. "Look down. Are you wearing shoes? What do they look like?"

In the vision I look down. I am wearing shoes. A rough, handmade leather pair, like something Robin Hood probably wore. *Robin Hood.* Just the thought makes me cringe. This is ridiculous. I can't do this. I sit up, pushing back the eye mask. I refuse to lead myself, or Gahl, through another regression in which I feel like I am just making things up.

"I'm sorry. I can't do this," I tell him.

"What is it you can't do?" Gahl asks.

"I don't know. I just feel like I'm making this stuff up."

"Yes, it can feel like that. It takes time to feel really comfortable. I think you should take the recording of our meditation home and practice on your own. Maybe you will feel less inhibited if you are alone."

I nod, feeling disappointed in myself, and worrying that Gahl is disappointed in me as well.

It will be two years before I feel ready to attempt another regression. Over the course of those two years all the things that Gahl predicted from my astrological chart come true. After my session with him I listened to the recording from my time in his office, making note of all the dates on which he claimed certain things would happen—travels and my book publishing date, other success and failures—and like clockwork, each event unfolds just as he said it would.

Could it all really be that simple? Could our fate really be written in the stars under which we were born?

I'm standing outside an ancient dusty city somewhere in the Middle East. I too am dusty and ancient. I am a man at the very end of his lifetime, in my seventies, at least. I stand at the edge of this city, knowing it is the home of my birth, but feeling reluctant to approach. It has been decades since I have set foot in this place.

"So do you enter?" a voice asks.

## After This

I sigh, feeling weary. "Yes," I reply. "I have to."

"Why do you have to?" the voice asks again.

"Because there is something I need to do before I die," I say.

"What do you have to do?"

I already know the entire story of this lifetime. The moment the regression began the whole thing unfolded in my mind. Not in the way a story unfolds, but in the way that you just know something, like the way you know a memory. I begin to walk Gahl through the story anyway.

It's been just over two years since I last sat in his office. I have given birth to the baby I was carrying when we first met, a little girl I named Juliette, after my friend Julie. I have also had a series of experiences that have finally led to feeling open to attempting another regression.

In the past two years I have seen countless mediums. I have danced in shaman circles, channeling my inner power animals and traveling to different realms. I have meditated and I have tried to commune with spirit guides, all of these experiences serving to help me finally relinquish the hold my rational mind has on such experiences. I just don't care anymore if I am making this stuff up, and even if I am, I have seen that there is validity in the experience one way or another.

So this time, when Gahl regresses me, I am right there. An old man in the ancient Middle East.

"So what is it you have to do?" Gahl asks, as I stand there in my vision, looking at the city before me.

"I have to get something to my daughter." And in the vision I begin to move forward. These visions move like dreams. One moment I'm standing outside the city; the next minute I'm inside its walls, in an old building, and I'm digging something up from beneath the floor of the room I'm in.

"Tell me what you're seeing," Gahl says.

"I'm in a room, digging up a vase out of the floor. I have to take it to my daughter."

"What is the significance of the vase?" Gahl asks.

"It's very valuable. I need to get it to her before I die."

"Where is your daughter? What can you tell me about her?"

The vision of a young woman in her twenties or thirties, with dark hair, swims into focus. She has small children around her.

"She is here in the city," I tell Gahl. "She thinks I'm dead. I fled the city many, many years ago."

"Hmm . . . ," he says. "I'd like to ask you now to visit a significant moment in this man's life that has to do with this vase."

Immediately the scene is grisly. I'm now in my thirties, physically fighting with another man. The man is my brother. The vase sits on the floor some distance away from us, and we are fighting over it. My hands are around my brother's neck. I am choking him in my fury and panic. I watch the life drain out of him and then the vision ends.

I describe the scene to Gahl and then tell him that after I killed my brother I buried the vase and fled the city, that I have spent the rest of my life since then in exile, wandering from city to city, living in complete solitude. I abandoned my wife and children without explanation, and now my daughter is grown with children of her own and I have returned to get this vase to her.

"Will you see her?" he asks.

"I don't think so. I just want to get this to her. It is a very valuable vase and it was always meant to provide for my family."

"Let's go back to the end of this man's life, then," Gahl says.

In the vision I am struggling to get to my daughter. I am literally at the end of my life, using my last bit of strength to make this journey. I make it to her doorstep and collapse, the vase in my hands. I die there, outside my daughter's door, without ever having seen her.

## After This

Gahl instructs me to leave the man's body and ascend into the clouds above. "Tell me, now that you can look back on this man's life, what was the lesson learned?"

I am still in a sedated state, under the blanket in Gahl's office chair, my eyes closed. I replay the life again in my mind.

"It was all in vain," I say. "I killed my own brother in order to give this vase to my family so that I could provide for them, but it was pointless. They didn't need the vase. They just needed me to be there for them."

"And what is the lesson there?" Gahl asks.

"The lesson is that I am more valuable than any object or achievement I could have provided. The lesson was to learn to see myself as enough."

---

Driving home from Gahl's office, through the threaded freeways that crisscross Los Angeles, I think about the regression, and the lesson of that man's lifetime. It's a lesson I myself have struggled with ever since my mother died.

Since the moment she was gone, I have struggled to see myself as valuable. When I lost my mother, I also lost the reflection of myself that she showed me on a daily basis, a reflection of a young woman who was loved and cared about and wanted.

Even the most important accomplishments of my lifetime have felt slightly hollow in her absence. Without the person who brought me into this world, I have struggled to feel like I am worthy of having a place in it.

I think about both of the past lives I have now experienced: one in which an entire lifetime was spent in grief, and another in which that lifetime was spent in exile over feeling worthless. In both instances I can see how these things relate to my life as it is now, the grief that has followed me into adulthood and the sense that my only value comes from what I achieve in this world.

Is this a lesson I must learn over and over until I get it right?

At home I page through Gahl's book *Cosmic Navigator*, searching for ways to unravel these past-life experiences I've now had. In the book he explains that our astrological chart is less a tool with which to see our future and more a contract we have made with our spiritual guides. Complaining about the way our lives are going is useless, he suggests. Accepting that the events that make up our lifetime are part of a grand plan to help us actualize our souls is truly the first step to achieving enlightenment.

Gahl's description of how we go about making these contracts is intriguing:

> We know from the accounts of people who have died clinically and then returned to life that when we die, our entire life flashes in front of our eyes. Reportedly, it feels like we relive our lives all over again. It sounds as if we download our lives from our body, which contains our memories in its cells, brain, and other organs, into the part of ourselves that is eternal. After completing this file transfer, we are welcomed into the Light by an entity that most mythologies call the psychopompus, or the guide of the souls. . . .
>
> According to many spiritual traditions, we have all made this journey from death to life and back again many times, and we will experience it again and again until we attain enlightenment. It goes something like this. After recovering from the shock of dying, we slowly begin to accept the fact that this round is done and we are about to begin anew. We meet a guide, who often appears in the guise of a relative. This benevolent *sherpa* of our soul leads us to a place where we can

review the file that we downloaded from our body and contemplate all that occurred in our life. Then, with the aid of our mentor, who is actually an ambassador of God, we identify the uncompleted trials and lessons that we probably ought to deal with in our next lifetime. Together with our guide, we figure out how best to do that. Should we be reborn a woman or a man, a Christian or a Jew, black or white, rich or poor?

I muse on Gahl's understanding of reincarnation. If I am to look at the two lives I've now been regressed to, I have to admit that they align with his philosophy. In both lifetimes I have placed value on external objects and success, rather than what I myself have to offer. What can I do in this lifetime to further learn this lesson? How can I make a better effort to accept the life I am living, rather than constantly struggle to make it something more than what it simply is?

It reminds me again of what the rabbi said in our meetings when I told him my fears about leaving my daughters behind. There is no sense in worrying about that, he told me. It is not in my hands what will happen to me or them. All I can do with this time here is my very best to be the best mother, the best writer, the best human possible.

I watch my girls growing bigger and learning more about the world every day. When I asked Gahl about free will versus destiny, he explained that although there is a plan, a contract, what we do with it is up to us. Therefore it is up to me—everyone, really—to just do our best with what we have.

But although I can accept that our fate is not necessarily in our hands, I'm not ready to fully embrace the notion of past lives. I keep twisting the experiences I had back and forth in my head, trying to make them fit into my clinical views of grief.

I return to what I found comforting, the idea that our paths are predestined. Even though it's not something I'm necessarily ready to believe, I'm interested in how exploring this notion can have therapeutic value.

I ponder what it would be like to ask my clients this question: What would it change for you to imagine that the events that have occurred in your life—the tragedies and losses, the successes and achievements—are part of a contract you made before you were even born?

I think that the most difficult part of the grief process is simply accepting the loss, and in this way I can see how at least considering the idea that our paths are predestined might alleviate the guilt and remorse and bouts of magical thinking that so often accompany grief.

Almost every client I've ever seen has expressed some level of regret for their actions surrounding the death of a loved one. In some cases, they simply regret not having been more present, and in others there are actual events or choices they wish they had handled differently. What if they didn't really have a choice at all? What if this was always the way it was going to happen? What if, like Gahl suggests, it was all determined before they were even born?

I've seen clients struggle so deeply with feelings of remorse that they enter into a path of magical thinking, going over and over the loss in their heads, trying to find something that could have prevented it. When this effort proves futile and all possible scenarios with which to refute the loss have been exhausted, then bargaining sets in. *I promise I'll never be mean to another person, never have judgmental thoughts. I'll quit my bad habits. I'll live a life of service. I'll do any and all of these things, if this person I love could just come back.*

Anger and sadness and depression come after that, but those are the paths that lead to the eventual acceptance of the loss. This person is gone and is not coming back. Your life looks different than you ever imagined and now you understand that there is nothing you can

## After This

do to change that fact. At first this acceptance is marked by anguish, but slowly you may find ways to see meaning and beauty in the loss, and this is often the moment in which you begin to heal in the midst of your grief.

So I wonder, even if someone does not believe wholeheartedly in reincarnation and divine contracts, what would it be like to imagine what it would mean for his or her life anyway? I wonder how it might help clients to look at the significant events that have shaped their existences and dwell on what they have learned from them.

In the year following my mother's death, and especially in the decades that have occurred since all the losses I have experienced, I have found myself strangely grateful for the experiences. Sometimes I have even wondered if I would take them back—if I would have my parents back—if it meant I would have to return to being who I was before they died.

Everything that I have been forced to learn about myself and the world as a result has been an incredible gift in so many ways. Their deaths have made me appreciate my life and my time with those I love in such a profound manner that I honestly do not know if I would have it any other way now, given the chance.

# Claire Bidwell Smith

Dear Vera and Jules,

My mother always told me to be an archaeologist. She dreamed of me being out in the world, far, far away, exploring all the things she never got a chance to. She wanted me to be an artist too, and all the time I was growing up she coaxed me into endless art classes, hanging my drawings and paintings all over the house with pride. And then there were the years of tennis classes that she enrolled me in, watching from the sidelines as I swayed back and forth, a racket in my hand, waiting for the tiny yellow ball to bounce my way.

But I didn't want to paint or draw. I wanted to write. And I didn't want to play tennis; I wanted to run. And I don't want to be an archaeologist, at least not in the sense she envisioned for me. Perhaps I'm an archaeologist now, of life and death and the psyche, but you will not find me in Africa, dusting off prehistoric bones at ancient cave sites.

Archaeology, and art, and tennis. Those were my mother's dreams, not mine. I understand why she had them for me, what she saw in me, what she wanted for me. I have similar desires for both of you. Vera, I see you as an artist, a singer, a performer, a fashion designer, always drawing from your fierce creativity and imagination. Jules, I see you working with animals, with people, as a doctor, maybe, moving through realms that require great compassion and concentration.

But who is to say what it is you will really want to do?

## After This

It takes some people all their lives to figure this out. They struggle with their identities in the face of what the world wants or expects from them. They get locked in, trapped by logistics and rules and formats, adhering to some idea of who they think they are supposed to be.

And so that's all I really want for you. I just want you to never feel stuck, to never feel deterred by the passion that pulls at you from within. I want you to feel utterly free to pursue your heart's desires, whatever those may be.

I feel lucky that when I brought home my drawings from art class, with little poems scribbled on the sides, my mother recognized that it was words, not sketches, that fed my soul. I'm lucky that when I told her I wanted to quit tennis and join the cross-country team, she cheered me on from those sidelines too. I'm lucky that when I threw myself into writing and told her that is what I wanted to be when I grew up, she let me wake her in the middle of the night to read my new poems to her.

I promise to support you in your quests and endeavors, if you promise to always be true to yourself, and your passions.

There are a great many things that will try to get in the way of you being who you are. There will be heartbreak and there will be loss and there will be accidents unforeseen, forks in the road you never could have anticipated. Let them shape you, rather than deter you. Let go of the frustration you'll experience, the anger that things are not what you thought they would be. Embrace the experiences, no matter how painful, and learn from them.

Every single painful experience I've had in my life has

served as a great lesson to help me understand myself and the world. For so long I struggled to see this. I felt resentful and bitter about the things that kept happening to me. I failed to see the radical ways in which these things were helping me to grow.

The quickest way through pain and regret is to let yourself flow into it for a time. Embrace it, own it, feel it, and you will discover more depths that life has to offer. You will see the world with fresh eyes each time you are dropped to your knees, and you will rise up again stronger and wiser and more grateful for who you are.

Let yourself be humbled, not destroyed. It is in our most fragile moments when we can truly learn who we are meant to be.

My only hope is that I will be here every time you fall, that I will be able to pick you up and dust you off, and set you on your feet again. But I know that is impossible. I won't always be here when you need me. But even when I'm not, just remember how much I love you, draw on that love inside you, hold on to it in your darkest moments, and you will find the strength to rise up on your own.

Life is worth living, my father said to me once in his final days. And he was right.

I love you always,

Mama

## Chapter Five

I'm not sure what I'm expecting, but the five-by-seven photograph in my hand simply looks like one that you would toss out of the stack you get back from the drugstore.

"Do you see that bright light right there in the center?" the woman who handed me the photo asks.

I nod, peering more closely. The photograph is of a kitchen window, taken at nighttime, and to me the bright light being referred to just looks like a reflection of the flash in the windowpane.

"Every photo I take has this same bright light," the woman continues, and her husband nods at me solemnly. Moments before handing me the photos she introduced herself as a ghost photographer.

"That's so unusual," I respond in regard to the photograph, hoping that my false enthusiasm isn't too obvious. I begin cutting up Vera's chicken fingers on a plate in front of me. It's an awkward task, as my younger daughter, three-month-old Juliette, is asleep in a baby carrier on my chest.

It is November 2012, and we're sitting in a banquet booth at the sixth annual Afterlife Conference in Phoenix, Arizona. I'm struck by the fact that I'm in Arizona again. This region is starting to feel like the new age center of the country, likely due to its strong Native American history and the large spiritual population of Sedona.

My husband, Greg, is leafing through our tablemate's stack of photos now, and I have to bite my lip to keep from laughing. I concentrate on feeding Vera her dinner and keeping her contained as we wait for the evening's keynote speaker, psychic medium Theresa Caputo, of the hit reality show *Long Island Medium*.

I have dragged my husband and daughters to this conference, promising them a fun weekend at the hotel pool while I attend two days of presentations and lectures about the afterlife. Trying to keep my skeptical husband, my wily toddler, and a fussy baby happy is going to be a feat. I can only imagine what the girls will think of their mom when they are old enough to realize all the weird adventures I subjected them to while researching this book.

A hushed murmur suddenly goes through the room as Theresa Caputo enters.

"Mama, I like her shoes," three-year-old Vera whispers, tugging on my shirtsleeve. I crane my neck to see, and watch as Caputo crosses the packed room. She is wearing four-inch glittery silver stilettos, the likes of which I have only ever seen on clichéd portrayals of strippers in bad movies.

"Yup, they're pretty amazing," I say to Vera. "Now eat your chicken fingers."

Vera busies herself with her food, making faces at her new playmate, the ghost photographer's five-year-old daughter, and Caputo addresses the room with a handheld microphone. I observe that in addition to the stilettos, Caputo is wearing a very short, tight dress that doesn't hide one bulge on her generous figure. Her white-blond hair is teased so high that, along with the heels, she's probably added a good eight inches to her height.

Theresa Caputo's show, *Long Island Medium*, was an instant hit

## After This

when it debuted one year ago on the TLC network. The series follows Caputo as she juggles her family and her clients in her day-to-day life on Long Island. In one episode that I saw, Caputo, while grocery shopping with her teenage daughter, felt compelled to confront a woman in the meat department about some messages she was receiving from the woman's deceased loved one. Caputo's daughter balked with embarrassment as her mother approached the stranger, but then her messages to the woman were so moving and healing that her daughter couldn't help but admire her.

It's an engaging premise, and scenes like the one in the grocery store are certainly compelling, but at this point I've seen enough mediums to be more than a little wary. At our banquet dinner Caputo begins to work the room just as John Edward did when I saw him. She begins by navigating through the tables, each person she walks toward looking up hopefully. She rattles off identifying characteristics about the spirit that is coming through to her.

"I've got a woman here," Caputo says in her heavy Long Island accent. "She died of something abdominal, like a stomach cancer or something. She's older, maybe seventies. Is this resonating with anyone?"

A woman in the back of the room raises her hand and speaks up, her voice shaky. "My mother died last year of pancreatic cancer."

"Yes, yes, I think she is here for you. She's showing me a garden. Lots of flowers. Did she have a garden or something?"

"Yes, she loved to garden. She grew the most beautiful roses," the woman says, desperation edging into her voice.

I glance across the table at Greg and he rolls his eyes. Again, I bite my lip to keep from laughing. It's not that I think this is funny—the opposite, really. But I find humor in watching an utter skeptic like Greg experience this stuff.

I tune back in to the dialogue with Caputo and the woman in

the back of the room. Caputo is telling her that her mother is at peace now, that she knows how loved she was. The woman is crying and holding the hand of the man seated next to her. Caputo backs away, heading toward another side of the room, her long fake fingernails clicking on the handle of the microphone.

We listen to Caputo go through a few more people, but Jules is fussing in her carrier and Vera is growing restless as well. Greg and I bid our tablemates good night and exit the banquet room, walking back to our room at the other end of the hotel.

"What did you think of Caputo?" I ask Greg.

He shakes his head and laughs. "You know how I feel about this stuff, Claire."

I laugh. "I know. But you liked James Van Praagh, right?"

He gives me a look. It's a simple one, but in a way it cuts to the heart of my dilemma about these mediums. Greg's look tells me that yes, he did like psychic medium James Van Praagh, whom we saw last summer, but that despite liking him, Greg does not know how to process the experience, so he has simply filed it away.

This is the problem I keep running up against with these mediums. I feel inconclusive about both John Edward and Theresa Caputo. They are both very good at working a room. They are funny and loud and commanding. They are a little intimidating and they are demanding in their direct approaches. But I cannot decide if their gifts are genuine or if they are just putting on a show, if perhaps they are just good at preying on vulnerable people.

However, James Van Praagh was a different story.

I first went to see Van Praagh in the summer of 2011. Greg and I drove down to Laguna Beach, where he hosts "spirit circles" on a monthly basis. We took our seats in the front row of a hotel conference room,

## After This

along with one hundred other participants who had each paid a hundred dollars to attend.

Along with John Edward, James Van Praagh has long been one of the biggest psychic mediums in this country. He is the author of dozens of best-selling books, all with titles like *Ghosts Among Us*, *Talking to Heaven*, and *Unfinished Business*. He also co–executive produced the CBS primetime series *Ghost Whisperer*, which was based on his life.

According to his website, Van Praagh was raised Roman Catholic and attended seminary school, where he claims he heard a message from a spirit telling him that "God is much bigger than these four walls." He majored in broadcasting and communication at San Francisco State University and then moved to Los Angeles, where an encounter with a psychic medium named Brian Hurst convinced him to pursue this work.

Van Praagh now travels the world, lecturing and doing large events where he communicates with spirits and relays messages to audience members. I didn't have very high expectations going into that first reading with him, but after my visits with Delphina and John Edward, I was left with more questions than answers. Like getting multiple opinions from different doctors, I was eager to see another medium so that I could continue forming my opinion.

That night Greg and I sat together and watched the room fill up with participants. Again, I felt a sense of protectiveness over all those who walked through the door, knowing that each person I saw was likely there because they had lost someone dear to them, and that each of them was likely hoping to receive a message.

After everyone had taken their seats, James Van Praagh entered the room and took hold of a wireless microphone. He's in his midfifties, stout and cheery in appearance. He greeted the room warmly and everything about his candor put me at ease. Openly gay, Van

Praagh is funny and self-deprecating. I could feel everyone around me relaxing as he talked about his background as a medium and what we could and could not expect from our session that evening.

"I work from a place of sacredness," he said. "Each of you in this room is a spirit, first and foremost. You are a spirit having a human experience. This place, earth, is a classroom. You are a student of human life and we come back here to learn different lessons that will help us grow spiritually. Some souls come back and experience things for eighty years, some come back for twenty, some souls are only here for days or hours, learning lessons in that short period of time, before they return to the source. It doesn't matter how you leave, because you really don't die."

I glanced over at Greg, wondering how he was taking this in. Raised in a very traditional Midwestern family, he hadn't been exposed to this kind of stuff much in his life, and I was curious as to how he was processing it. He looked relaxed and interested, and I was reminded of how much I appreciate his openness to the woo-woo stuff I'm continually subjecting him to.

Van Praagh continued. "We come back here with family and friends, people we've lived many lifetimes with before. As Shakespeare said, 'Life is a stage and we are all players.'"

I looked around the room and the entire audience seemed engaged, listening to Van Praagh. While I didn't yet feel prepared to fully put stock in his view of spirits and the human experience, it was nonetheless an appealing notion to me. I was also appreciative of his approach. John Edward had offered no real framework for us to understand our experience with him in the hotel that night when he gave readings.

"If you can get to a place where you can just be objective when something really happens, instead of reacting . . . if you can stop, take a breath, and stand back, ask yourself, *What am I learning here?*

*What is this situation teaching me?* You get through the lessons much easier if you can do this. But again, it's a process."

As I listened to Van Praagh, I thought about the various ways I'd reacted to my parents' deaths. For many years I'd felt like a victim of my circumstances. I'd felt cheated and robbed of the kind of life I'd thought I was supposed to have. It took me a long time to stop moving through life as though I were constantly under attack, and to learn to focus on positive moments, to try to embrace the challenges life presented, and learn from them, just as Van Praagh suggested.

He began to prepare us for the night's reading. "The best way to experience tonight is to be very open to whatever happens. As we share the space with spirits we need to be open and relaxed so that they can come in. It's usually the husband who was dragged here by his wife who gets a reading."

The room laughed and I elbowed Greg. On the way down to the reading Greg had speculated who, if anyone, might come through for him. The only significant people he'd ever lost were his grandparents. I was, of course, hoping to hear from Julie or my parents, but I took a breath and tried to just be open, like Van Praagh suggested.

"Here's what we're going to do. When I come to you with a message—and I never know from night to night what's going to happen—I'll see the person standing behind you, or in my mind's eye I'll see a scene taking place. Sometimes I see a hospital scene. If they died in the street I'll see that. I get names, ages. If you think this person is for you, please raise your hand and acknowledge it. It can be someone you don't expect, so listen carefully. You may be waiting to hear from your dead mother, but instead your cousin three times removed who you only met twice comes through."

People around the room laughed nervously. Despite what Van Praagh said about being open, I knew that it would be difficult for many of the people there to let go of their expectations for the night.

Finally Van Praagh dimmed the lights and led us through a relaxation meditation. Again, I appreciated this kind of opener. It seems nearly impossible to walk out of your regular, day-to-day life and right into a reading without taking some time to relax and reflect on what you are about to experience. In the cases of visiting John Edward and Delphina, I had taken my own moments of meditation before the readings.

Finally Van Praagh began. That night with Greg neither of us was read, but we both watched with awe as he brought forth incredible details and images to the people he did read. And with each reading, I was impressed with the way he approached the audience members with enormous amounts of respect and compassion, always working to find a healing message within the context of connecting them with a deceased loved one.

We both left that night feeling warm and positive, my skeptic husband chattering to me the entire drive home about the uncanny connections that had been made that night. However, it would be a couple of months later, on another visit to Van Praagh, that he would really make my jaw drop.

"Okay, I've got a sister here. And she has a sister in the audience. She passed over and I feel like it's a cancerous condition. There's blood being given, IVs, a hospital."

I nudge my friend Liz, who is seated next to me. I can't believe she hasn't raised her hand yet. This sounds like it could absolutely be her older sister, Jen, who died three years earlier.

Then again, it's the very first reading of the night, and even I can't quite believe that, out of the hundred people in the room, the first reading might be for her.

Liz and I met in preschool when we were four years old. We've

## After This

been friends almost our entire lives, particularly close during our high school years and our early twenties. She knew my parents better than any other friend of mine, and often I've felt that she's the closest thing I have to a sister, Liz being the only other keeper of memories that might have belonged solely to me after my parents were gone.

In 2007 Liz's sister died of cancer. She'd been diagnosed only three years before, at age thirty-two. Her daughter was just two years old. I'll never forget holding Jen's hand as she cried after Liz's wedding ceremony, when she was too sick to partake in the dance party, having used her last strength to make it through the vows.

Jen's death rocked Liz's small family, and in the past three years my sweet friend has been overtaken with grief over the loss of her sister. Liz and her husband and two children recently moved to Long Beach, forty minutes south of where I live, in Santa Monica, and after my initial visit to James Van Praagh I called her to tell her that I thought she should try it out. She was skeptical, never having considered seeing a medium, but she was open to it and agreed to join me.

As we drove down together, I promised that his approach to all this was very gentle and that I felt sure it would be a good experience. Nonetheless I felt protective of my friend, worried that it might exacerbate her grief, rather than soothe it.

I nudge Liz again, and she finally raises her hand, catching Van Praagh's eye as he looks around the room for the sister of the spirit he is communicating with.

"My sister did pass. She had cancer," Liz says in a soft voice.

Van Praagh zeros in on her, nodding. "What's your name?"

"Liz."

My heart is racing, and I'm glad I'm recording this on my phone.

"Liz. May I come to you?" he asks, and again I feel appreciative of his gentle manner, after having felt barraged by John Edward during my own reading.

"Sure," she says.

"Your sister passed from a cancerous condition. Did she go into the hospital for treatments? For chemo? For IV treatments?"

"Yeah, chemo. I went with her."

"Do you know a Betty? Is that your name? You're Elizabeth? Is there another Elizabeth?" he asks.

"My niece was given my name. My sister's daughter," Liz says.

"Your sister's daughter?" he asks.

"Her name is Ashley Elizabeth."

"She has a daughter that's still walking around this earth? So you share the name of this girl? I also understand that there's another child as well?"

"Well," Liz says. "My sister was pregnant with her second when she was diagnosed and she had to terminate the pregnancy."

I remember Liz calling to tell me about Jen's cancer, crying into the phone about how Jen would have to abort her second child so that she could begin treatment immediately. There are tears in my eyes, listening to my friend going over these details in a room full of people.

At the same time I wonder if it might be healing in some way. Some of the most powerful moments I've ever witnessed in the grief work I've done have been when people were able to openly share their stories.

"I knew it," Van Praagh says. "I knew there were two. Okay, so she's unsure about coming close to me. I have to tell you this. So as I'm speaking to you, Liz, I'm trying to let her know I'm cool. She's just unsure of this whole thing."

The people around us laugh a little, and Liz smiles.

"Do you like to read all the time?" he asks.

## After This

"I did," Liz says, and when I hear her say this it breaks my heart. All her life Liz was an avid bookworm, but ever since Jen died she has lost interest in almost everything, except her own children. Liz found out she was pregnant with her first the month after Jen died, never getting to share the experience of motherhood with her sister.

"Your mind is always in a book or magazine, all the time. She's acknowledging you reading all the time," Van Praagh says. "Do you have any books of hers?"

"I have a book she gave me as a present," Liz admits.

"And did you see that book just recently?"

"Yeah, I looked at it before I came tonight," she says, and there is utter stillness in the room, everyone listening raptly, necks craning to better see my friend.

"So she's just acknowledging the book. That she was with you when you looked at that book. She's acknowledging that she wrote you something in that book. She wrote you a little note. Is that right?"

"Yes."

"Yes, thank you. And I know you said to her, 'If you come here tonight mention that book.'"

"I didn't say it out loud," Liz says, surprise edging her voice, and there is a collective gasp in the room.

"No, you didn't," Van Praagh says. "You said it in your mind. She received that thought. You sent her that thought. And it's because of your openness that she's here. And it's because of your openness that you want to know if this is real. She's here to tell you that this *is* real. She's here to tell you that there is no such thing as death. Your sister here next to me is wondering how I know all of this if I'm not dead yet. She doesn't quite get it."

I can picture Jen as Van Praagh is talking. She was six years older than Liz, always the cool big sister we looked up to. I look at the empty space next to him, and wonder if she is really standing right there, invisible to the rest of us.

"Who is Teresa?" he asks then.

"Um, her nurse was Mary Teresa."

"Your sister wants to give her love to her. She wants to thank her. And didn't she go to the memorial service?"

"Yes," Liz says, and there is another small gasp from the people around us.

"Yes. Because she's acknowledging her. I don't know if she had a gold pin. Do you understand about the gold pin that this nurse wore? The pin had a cross in it? Or, like, a circle with a cross in it?"

"In the Jewish religion, when you're buried, the family wears a black circle, a ribbon," Liz explains.

"A ribbon?"

"Yeah, and we all had them with gold pins."

"Thank you," Van Praagh says. "I know. I see it. Now that she's cool with me, she's kind of getting the vibe of it. And she sees the reaction within you. When we understand what they're saying our auric field changes colors. You have a sense of knowingness."

Van Praagh addresses the room as he says this last part, and right then an audience member gets up and walks past him to use the bathroom. He takes a noticeable step backward, shaking his head.

"Ohh. She just walked right through our connection," he says, referring to the woman who went to the bathroom. "When I read you I connect a cord to you. So when someone walks through it . . . I didn't tell you that. It's not her fault. . . ."

He takes a moment then, seeming to collect himself and tune back in. Finally he speaks again.

"I feel like there is someone else now, on the other side, with short black bangs. Not sure if it's your mother or your mother's mother. There's an old photograph of her. I know you were looking at photos."

"Yes," Liz says again, and I continue to marvel at the reading.

"Was it a grandmother of yours?"

"My mother's mother passed away," she says. Liz's mother, Lenore, always had a strange sadness about her, something I noticed even as a little girl. Liz attributed it to her having lost her mother at a young age.

"Was there a Ruth? Rose?"

"I don't know," Liz says.

"I'm gonna stay with Ruth. February. She was born in February," Van Praagh says.

"I don't know."

"Look up a grandmother in February. February twenty-fourth." Van Praagh takes another moment, seeming to be listening to something none of the rest of us can hear. "I know you have some boxes of your sister's. Belongings of hers. And you don't know where to put them. You have not yet gone through them. Are you aware that she gave you some items to save for her daughter? Do you have any jewelry that you're going to give to her daughter?"

"I don't, but my dad has it," Liz says.

"She's just acknowledging that some jewelry was put away, and that I know that there is going to be a wedding one day, and that she wants her daughter to wear whatever this is. I know there are pearl earrings as well."

"Yes," Liz says.

"She wants her to wear them at her wedding. She's screaming it at me. She wants her to wear them at her wedding. And a necklace as well. It's a gold chain thing."

"Yeah," Liz says. I don't know anything about the jewelry, but I do know that Liz wouldn't acknowledge it if it weren't true.

"I know. Ruth Ann! That's the name," Van Praagh suddenly says enthusiastically. "She's yelling Ruth Ann! She goes back in time. I see an old type of desk. A secretary desk. Is that what they call them?" He pauses again, and then continues. "Your father's still here, still alive? I want to talk about Dad. He's been coughing lately."

"Yeah," Liz says.

"I'm worried about—your sister is screaming at me—'I'm worried about his cough, his cough, his cough.' And I feel lungs are congested. His heart is paining. There's also a sense of him wishing he could have done something for his little girl." Van Praagh is barreling through all these details now and we're all just nodding along at this point. "Liz, do you know about drawing cartoons?"

"I used to draw them," she says. Liz has been an artist for as long as I can remember, always drawing.

"I know you did," Van Praagh says. "She's showing me cartoons, that you used to do them as kids, or you'd show them to her. And I know you still have some of these."

"Yeah."

"I know you were looking at some of these recently," he says with conviction.

"My mom just brought them over to my house."

Here Van Praagh runs through a few more vague scenes and images that come to him—a gold bracelet, a grandfather—none of it seeming to resonate with Liz all that much. And then he asks, "Did you have bunk beds?"

"No. But my husband and I were just talking about getting them for our kids because our third is coming."

"Ohh," Van Praagh says with a smile. "Do you want to know what it is?"

"Go ahead," Liz says.

"I think it's a boy. I think it's a boy."

"Oh, really? Okay."

In fact, just a few weeks after this reading, Liz will find out that she is indeed due with a boy.

"I know your sister is helping you. And can I just say that a part of her is going to be with that baby? An aspect of her is going to be in that baby. And I know you want to know that." I can see tears form in Liz's eyes when he says this.

"She's a teacher," Van Praagh says next.

"She was," Liz replies. Jen taught special-needs children in an elementary school.

"She was a teacher here on this earth?"

"Yes."

"Well, she's also teaching over there. She's helping motherless girls. Girls who come over here without mothers," he says, and now tears come into my own eyes.

"A couple more things and then I want to move on. Your sister is saying, 'I want to thank you for all you did for me. Thank you for bringing me to different places.' And someone rubbed lotion on her back."

"I did," Liz says. I think about how devoted Liz was to Jen's care those last months, and what it must be like for her to hear this message of gratitude from her sister.

"She wants to thank you," he says. Then he takes a look at Liz for a moment before he speaks again. "God bless you. You're fine. You're healthy. You need to realize that your sister is with you more now than she was able to be with you on this earth. One more thing. Was there a three-ring, loose-leaf binder that you found that belonged to her?"

"Yeah," Liz says.

"Thank you. She just wanted you to know that she knew." Van

Praagh takes a deep breath here and turns back to the room. I reach for Liz's hand. She is shaking a little. I am too.

Can mediums really communicate with the deceased? This is the question posed by Dr. Julie Beischel in a series of scientific studies conducted in her lab at the Windbridge Institute.

I listen to Dr. Beischel's presentation with interest at the Afterlife Conference in Phoenix. I have asked myself this same question many times since my visits to John Edward, Delphina, and James Van Praagh. In all three cases, the information the mediums brought forth was so uncanny—details they could not have known previously, nor could they have distinguished them simply by looking at me (or my friend Liz)—that I have been left with many questions.

Still reluctant to believe that a medium is truly connecting with a deceased individual on "the other side," I have wondered if perhaps the mediums have psychic capabilities that enabled them to read my mind, drawing forth information based on my own personal memories, which they have somehow gained access to. Although this also seems unbelievable, it's somehow more plausible than the idea of them actually communicating with the dead.

Dr. Julie Beischel is in her late thirties, smart, and businesslike. She has a PhD in pharmacology and toxicology from the University of Arizona, served as a postdoctoral fellow in mediumship and survival research, and is codirector of the VERITAS Research Program at the University of Arizona. In 2008 she cofounded the Windbridge Institute, an independent research organization consisting of a community of scientists who investigate human potential as it relates to paranormal capabilities, particularly in correlation to psychic mediums and bereavement.

The studies Dr. Beischel presents on PowerPoint on a large screen

## After This

in the auditorium at the conference are complex. I flash back to my high school science classes and find myself trying to remember how blind studies work.

In her presentation Dr. Beischel explains how she conducted a series of controlled studies in which she gave several Windbridge-approved mediums the names of deceased individuals (referred to as discarnates) offered by Windbridge-approved participants (referred to as sitters). She did not allow the mediums to have any direct contact with the sitters, giving them only the first name of the deceased individual through a third party.

To further ensure the validity of the study, the medium was given two different names at one time, each discarnate belonging to a different individual sitter. The medium then offered up information in reaction to each name. This information was passed back to the sitter, who received the information for both names, not knowing which was his or her deceased individual. The sitter was then asked to score both on an itemized list, give the whole reading a numerical score, and pick which discarnate was his or hers.

Dr. Beischel tells us that the mediums were never given feedback about how the readings went. This controls for precognition, or looking into the future. I sit there at my little table at the conference, trying to wrap my head around this idea. Basically she's saying that it's possible that the mediums could be using psychic capabilities to look into the future and view the results of the reading in order to give accurate details. "It seems implausible that they're looking into the future, because we're not going to give them the results," Dr. Beischel explains.

According to her studies, the data demonstrates that mediums are reporting accurate and specific information. Dr. Beischel admits that the proxy sitter makes it challenging, but certain elements that usually cause skepticism are eliminated. For instance, since it is a cold reading, the medium can't just be reading the sitter's body language. And there also can't be reader bias based on wanting the information to be true. Dr. Beischel says that when she compares target scores with the decoy scores, they are indeed higher. She feels that even though you can't control all the components, it is still pretty definitive proof.

"These mediums are reporting information that is correct and specific," she announces.

Following the conference I'll go on to read a lot of Dr. Beischel's studies and numerous published books, and even follow up with her by phone. Her research is fascinating, and seems to be the only kind being done in this country. She tells me that there is very little funding for this sort of thing, and describes further studies and work she would like to do if she had more money.

Julie Beischel's studies are meticulously outlined in her book *Among Mediums: A Scientist's Quest for Answers*. Although it's written largely for the layperson, I again found it challenging to wrap my head around some of her studies. However, I wasn't surprised to read in the opening chapters that her mother had committed suicide. It seems that everyone who is drawn to this field has been touched by loss in some way.

Dr. Beischel's presentation becomes the highlight of the conference for me, her scientific efforts counterbalancing all the tarot card readers and ghost photographers floating around. When we break for lunch, I find Greg and Vera and Jules at the pool. We grab some food and join a table of conference participants. Everyone is chatting with each other and I realize that we are sitting at a table of mediums, past-life therapists, and a woman who works with angels. I concentrate on getting my toddler to eat and I muse on how funny this all seems, and yet also how serious. So many of these people seem utterly freaky to me, yet presentations like Dr. Beischel's lend credibility to this being an important part of the grief process.

## After This

There is a sudden buzz around us as Dr. Eben Alexander walks among the tables. His book *Proof of Heaven*, about a near-death experience, became an instant best seller when it debuted earlier this year, and I take this as further evidence that there is more to all this. There is an obvious hunger in our culture for a better understanding about death, a yearning to know what happens next.

After lunch I bid my little family good-bye for the afternoon and return to my seat in the conference room to attend the lecture and presentation by Dr. Alexander. I read his book before the conference and am curious to hear him speak. I watch him take the stage. Tall, dressed in jeans and sport coat, he is smiling warmly. I particularly like him already, after an encounter the evening before, when he took the time to coo over Juliette.

Dr. Alexander projects a calmness that I envy. He stands behind the podium, surveying the room for a moment before he speaks, and then he leans in to the microphone. Just then it goes on the fritz, emitting a strange frequency, and a loud electronic whining fills the room. The audience begins to clap and hoot. "Spirit, spirit!" the people around me yell, seemingly convinced that an entity has taken over the PA system before Dr. Alexander has had a chance to speak.

He chuckles as a tech adjusts the microphone, and then he begins to tell us about the experience he outlines in his book. Dr. Alexander was a seasoned neurosurgeon in North Carolina when he fell into a rare meningitis-induced coma in 2008. In his book he recounts that during his coma he experienced a spiritual awakening when he visited an otherworldly realm.

According to medical data, Alexander was technically brain-dead during his coma, but during that time he claims to have visited another realm, where he met angels and spirits and felt a unifying love that convinced him that there is consciousness beyond death. In fact, his main proof, he tells us, is not so much the science behind his experience, but that he met a woman on his journey who later turned out to be a sister, whom he had not previously known about.

Throughout his presentation I envy his conviction. I want so badly to believe in his experience, to believe that when my parents died, when Julie died, when Liz's sister died, when *anyone* dies, this is what they go through—a peacefulness, a knowing that life is not just in these human bodies, that we go on and return to something much larger. Dr. Alexander is utterly convinced that there is more than just these lives we are living right now, that death is not an end, but rather a beginning.

After the presentation I chat with him for a while at the book-signing table. I ask him if he feels there is a particular religion here on earth that resonates most strongly with his experience, and he replies no. He tells me that he feels any religion that is not exclusive with its doctrines is wonderful. And last, he tells me that *God* is too small, too restricting a word for what he experienced.

"How does someone like me find this same peace you've found, without having a near-death experience?" I ask him.

Eben Alexander smiles at me, his eyes crinkling. "It's not easy," he says. "Meditation is one of our most useful tools. But also just accepting that feeling of knowing."

On the drive home from Arizona with Greg and the girls I find myself thinking about the night my father died, about staring down at his body and for just a moment knowing, really *knowing*, in that way Dr. Alexander described, that we are not just these bodies.

At one point during her presentation Dr. Julie Beischel discussed a study she had done that showed that a positive meeting with a psychic medium could have stronger healing effects on the grief process than traditional psychotherapy. She took a moment to poll the audience. "How many of you feel that seeing a psychic medium has helped you with your grief?"

Almost every hand in the audience went up, including the hand of the woman seated next to me. Earlier that morning this woman had told me that she lost her teenage son last year, and that her husband was steeped in denial and grief, but that she had taken a different tack, delving into this world and finding it healing. Her hand still in the air, she looked over at me and smiled.

Before exploring these psychic medium sessions, I would never have considered recommending that one of my clients visit a medium. Prior to my experiences with John Edward, Delphina, and James Van Praagh, I assumed that all mediums were likely quacks, and that seeing a medium when you are grieving is a sure sign of denial and desperation. But all that has changed now.

I think back to Liz and her experience with Van Praagh. Three years after that visit, I ask her to share her thoughts with me. The night of the reading we were both too stunned to really process our thoughts, and I'm curious how the experience settled for her. This is what she reports.

"I remember feeling so surprised by the whole reading and how it happened. Jen was the first one to come through and I just couldn't believe it was really her there. I knew the chances were so slim, so I didn't want to get my hopes up that she would come through. But he kept saying, 'Anyone? Anyone?' And you finally nudged me and said, 'Raise your hand!'

"The specifics were enough to convince me. I mean, I already believed, I think. I always felt like there was something more, and I always wondered where she was and if she was okay, and what was she doing, and could she see me, could she hear me, was she with me. And now I know.

"The book—there is no way he could have known about that. I

was alone in my house when I looked at it. I didn't speak any words out loud. It was the last thing I did before I walked out of the house and we got into the car to drive to the reading.

"She had to have been there with me, and again with him, with us in that room. That alone makes me believe. And her second child—I mean, how . . . how could he have known that?

"Some of the things, I still don't know what they are—Ruth Ann, not a clue. The part about the gold pin and Mary Teresa. Not sure. I don't remember her wearing a gold pin. Maybe she did. Maybe she had one on at the funeral; I don't know because the majority of that day is a blur. Maybe I said the stuff about the black ribbon and gold pin to make it fit. But I do believe what he said about her. I mean, if you are a skeptic and looking at it, he had a fifty-fifty chance of getting some of that stuff right—Mary Teresa at the funeral, me having a baby boy. But those things ended up being true.

"Nothing else really came to me after. I remember feeling it all swirling inside and in my head for weeks. I wanted to see him or another medium again and hear more. I never did, but I would love to again.

"Going to the reading definitely helped my grief process. I felt a little better and less unsure after. I felt like maybe I could stop wondering so much about her and where she was, how she was. I felt more peaceful about her death, and maybe the gaping hole didn't feel so big. I remember, after she died, wondering when, if ever, it wouldn't hurt so much, when would I stop wanting to die. How many years would it take to wake up and feel normal and not gutted? How did people ever go on and live normally? I wanted to scream. And until that reading, I wondered, daily, where she was. How was she? Could she see me? Could I feel her? Was I imagining things or was she with me?

"After seeing James Van Praagh, I felt a little more peaceful about the whole thing, and I was finally able to let go a little bit, I think. Just heal a little bit. It doesn't lessen the pain of losing her, but it did help to lessen the pain of not knowing. Every day she's gone is one more day away from our time together, but it's also one day closer until I can hopefully see her again, and I am hopeful that I will. His reading helped me stop wondering so much and stop feeling so lost."

When I hear these things from Liz, I cannot help but cry. When you see someone you love go through something like this, all you want to do is ease the pain for her. To think that this one session with James Van Praagh had such a profound effect on her grief astounds me, and I find myself seriously considering whether this is a more acceptable tool for coping with loss. I can already think of several of my clients who would benefit from having a positive medium experience like the one Liz had.

The bottom line is that grief is a reflection of how much we love someone. I believe that trying to reconcile the loss of that person in our hearts and our day-to-day lives can feel impossible at times. And so finding ways, no matter how far-fetched, to feel connected to that person is the very thing that can enable us to move forward, and to heal.

## Claire Bidwell Smith

Dear Vera and Jules,

It's Friday evening and I've just put you both to sleep in my bed and I'm sitting on the patio, drinking a glass of wine.

Some friends came for dinner tonight. I made macaroni and cheese and we had rocky road ice cream for dessert, and you kids bounced around the house all night like lunatics, playing with your dolls and dressing the cats in tutus.

Over the past couple of years since Jules has come into our lives I've watched you both grow and bond, and it's been utterly mysterious and entrancing to watch your relationship flourish.

You are remarkable little creatures, so full of life and passion and creativity. You fill my heart with love on the deepest level imaginable and I simply cannot imagine existing without you.

Vera, you turned five last month. You are so grown-up all of a sudden, with your lanky body and long blond hair, your fierce opinions and strong will. You are a rebellious girl, never listening to me or your father, always having to do things your way, or finish something you've gotten involved in, throwing fits if we drag you away.

But you're sensitive too. You cry easily, and I fear that you're going to spend a great many years making life harder than it needs to be. You're reluctant to try new things or venture out of your comfort zone. You're hesitant to follow our suggestions, so bullheaded about doing it your way. I think one day you'll find it easier to just relax into the flow, to let life be what it is, rather than what you want it to be.

Vera, you are my true soul mate. The love we have for each other is unparalleled, and I fret often about what you would ever do without me. I know that you will find your way eventually, but it's going to mean letting go of always being in control. I just want you to know that the love we share is so ancient and deep that I will always be with you. I am part of you. I am you. I always will be.

And sweet Jules, oh, my dear little one, you are a creature wholly unto yourself. You are fiercely determined to be part of this world, but you have nothing to fear. You are so full of love and light and laughter, the world can't help but love you back and open every door to you. You're so concerned with keeping up with everything and everyone around you, but I think that will fade and you will eventually settle into yourself.

Jules, when I see you peaceful and secure, at play, or communicating with one of your many beloved animals, I know that you will be most yourself when you get quiet and slow down.

I utterly adore you, Jules, but in many ways I feel like we are still getting to know each other. We are not the same. And you're not quite your father either. But you are here and you are brave and beautiful and so hungry for all that the world has to offer.

Never doubt my love for you, Jules. I think sometimes it will seem that Vera gets more attention or has a stronger connection with me, but oh, sweet one, you are teaching me more about how to be at peace in the world than anyone ever has. I will love you through the sands of time and back. If it feels like we never met before now, there will never again be a time when it will feel like we do not know each other.

So girls, right now in this moment, there is one thing I want for you above all others.

I want you to always love and take care of each other. You will surely have fights and disagreements, you'll hurt each other's feelings and loathe each other at times, but all you have to do to get through those moments is accept each other as the entirely different people you are.

You both emerged from my body, exactly three years apart, with golden hair and big blue eyes. But you are not each other. You are, in fact, so incredibly different. You will walk different paths and perceive the world in different ways, just as the world will receive you in different ways.

Remember that, work to accept it, and above all, look out for each other. Take care of each other. Love each other for all your differences and all the things that draw you together. Your sisterhood is a great, great gift. You will understand each other and rely on each other in ways that you never could with another soul. Respect each other and always return to gratitude for each other's existence.

I love you both to the moon and back. I always will, no matter what you do, where you go, or when you come back. I'll be with you every step of the way, guiding you and loving you and holding you. Never, ever doubt it.

With all my heart,

*Mama*

# Chapter Six

I open my eyes and look around the room at the twelve women facing me. We are seated on mats in a yoga studio in Ojai, California, where I am hosting my first grief retreat. All the women in this room are here because they lost someone—a mother, a sister, a child, a spouse. I watch them blink their eyes open and look around as well.

We have been meditating as a group for the past five minutes. "How was that for everyone?" I ask the room at large.

One woman raises her hand. "It was hard," she says. "I couldn't get rid of all the thoughts going through my head. Things I have to do when I get home, grocery lists and stuff. I just couldn't make my mind get quiet."

"The goal isn't necessarily to make your mind completely quiet," I say. "At least, not at first. The goal is to begin to become aware of your thoughts. To recognize that they are just thoughts, and that we don't have to attach to them. When we attach to them we feel emotions, so depending on what the thought is, it is followed with an emotion like anxiety or sadness, or even happiness. When we can begin to detach from our thoughts a little, we can find ways to get a grip on our emotions. This is particularly useful in the grief process."

As the words leave my mouth, it's like I'm having an out-of-body experience. Suddenly I'm floating above the room, looking down at myself and the other women. I see myself from the outside, a serene thirty-five-year-old woman, poised on her mat, lecturing to a group of people about the benefits of meditation.

Tears of gratitude come into my eyes at the scene, remembering myself a decade ago, when I was lost and grieving my mother's death in my early twenties. Back then I never thought I would find my way to the other side of grief, but I have, and this is what it looks like. Before I open my eyes again I make a silent wish that all the women seated around me are able to have a moment like this one sometime in the not-too-distant future.

"Okay," I say to the group. "Let's try again. This time for ten minutes."

My co-facilitator at the retreat, therapist and yoga instructor Thea Harvey, chimes in. "Before we begin again, I want all of you to picture a big, blue sky. Now picture puffy white clouds floating across it. The sky is your mind and each cloud that goes by is a thought. Let them just float by. Acknowledge that they're there, but don't attach to them. Just let them keep passing. You don't have to clear the sky entirely of clouds, but just try not to focus on them as much this time."

"So we shouldn't, like, climb up on one of the clouds and get comfortable?" a young woman named Ruth jokes, and we all laugh in response. Ruth has been a client of mine for the past two years, ever since her mother died. During that time I've watched her transform from the shattered individual she was when she first came to see me into someone strong, compassionate, and curious about life.

In my work I find myself constantly struck by how easily grief can destroy a person. Even though I've lived through it myself, on multiple occasions, it's different when you witness someone else go through it.

## After This

When we lose someone we love, suddenly nothing fits anymore. Who we thought we were is now a jumbled mess of memories and hopes we once had, for a future that now looks completely different. When we lose someone close to us we are forced to reevaluate our entire identities. We must figure out who we are now that this person is gone, and the experience can be overwhelming.

The first time I tried meditation was in the spring of 2007. I was twenty-eight years old and I had reached a crossroads in my life. My father had been gone for almost four years; my mother, for ten. I found that I could no longer continue to dwell in my grief, letting life just go on around me. I knew that it was time for me to pick up and begin moving forward again, but I wasn't sure what that looked like. I struggled to find meaning and purpose in my existence, and every time I thought about the bigger picture of my life, I felt overwhelmed and often filled with anxiety.

Either I was dwelling in the past, constantly thinking about what life had been like, or I was drowning in fears about the future, obsessing over what my life was *supposed to* look like, as opposed to how it actually did.

I'd begun doing yoga the year before and found it very grounding. I found that an hour-long class helped me focus on the present moment, rather than my usual obsessing over the past or future, and that I walked out of each session with a peacefulness I hadn't felt in years. Upon remarking as much to a friend of mine, he suggested I try a formal meditation practice, and recommended a teacher who could help me.

That's how I found myself in a little apartment in Westwood once a week, sitting opposite a woman named Juliette, who helped me learn to meditate. Juliette's apartment was sparse and clean, and each week we sat facing each other on little meditation pillows, so close that I could almost feel her breath when I closed my eyes.

Juliette began each session by talking to me about vipassana meditation, an ancient practice that originated in India thousands of years ago. Vipassana is also a technique used in the Buddhist practice of mindfulness, the art of learning to immerse yourself in the present moment.

Despite knowing these things, and despite hearing about the constant benefits of such a practice, I felt vipassana meditation to be nearly impossible in the beginning. Every time I closed my eyes my mind would go wild. I would try to focus on the feeling of my breath as it came through my nostrils, but instead I would just find myself bombarded by to-do lists, phone calls I needed to make, and bills I needed to pay. When I was able to clear those things away, then more abstract thoughts would take their place—insecurities, fears, random health concerns.

Before I knew it Juliette was ringing her little bell softly, signaling the end of our meditation, and I had gotten nowhere close to emptying my mind of thoughts. I would blink my eyes open and then we would discuss how it had gone. After that we would start all over again, each meditation lasting longer than the previous one.

In the moments when I was able to get past the mundane thoughts and the abstract ones, I would think I was getting close to finding serenity, but then my mind would throw a curveball at me, dredging up an old memory, usually something I hadn't thought of in years and years, and dragging me into a tailspin of emotion.

But the thing was this: What I realized as the weeks went on in Juliette's little apartment was that I was becoming *aware* of my thoughts, perhaps for the first time. Prior to these sessions I had never given, well . . . *thought* to my thoughts. They had always just come and gone, dominating my days and shaping my emotional landscape.

## After This

It had never occurred to me to even attempt to disengage from them. I would wake up in the morning and a thought of my dead mother would send me into a spiral of loneliness and abandonment before I had even climbed out of bed.

But suddenly I was learning that I could detach from that thought. I could focus on the present moment instead, the sunshine and ocean air coming through the window, the feeling of my body healthy and strong and rested, and then I could rise peacefully and go about making my coffee and planning my day.

This realization changed everything, and it is something that has stayed with me ever since, informing my days and the work I do with clients, and leading me, in fact, to the very moment in the yoga studio in Ojai on the grief retreat.

Buddhist teachings tell us that suffering is due to attachment, and that attachment comes from desire. The reason we experience pain in our lives is because we attach to people and places and outcomes, to things we desperately want but cannot always have. We are urged to let go, to loosen our grip on everything around us, to focus on the present moment, and only then will we be able to find peace.

It's a practice and a belief, like most spiritual notions, that is easier said than done. How do we release the desire for certain outcomes? How do we let go of our grief when we lose someone we love? How do we relinquish our fears of the future? I often worry that in doing so, I'll lose some part of my humanity. Isn't it exactly these emotions, this desire to experience life, that make us who we are?

Ultimately, I believe there is a balance to be sought, that learning to detach from our thoughts when they are driving us into an unwanted emotional place can be profoundly helpful. But I also think that honoring the emotional process of any life experience is important as well. We are human creatures, after all, and love—and all the pain that can sometimes come with it—is the driving force behind most of our actions.

However, Buddhist views are some of the most peaceful ones I've found when trying to understand and accept death.

In his book *No Death, No Fear*, contemporary Buddhist teacher Thich Nhat Hanh writes:

> Our greatest fear is that when we die we will become nothing. Many of us believe that our entire existence is only a life span beginning the moment we are born or conceived and ending the moment we die. We believe that we are born from nothing and that when we die we become nothing. And so we are filled with fear of annihilation.

He goes on to explain:

> The Buddha has a very different understanding of our existence. It is the understanding that birth and death are notions. They are not real. The fact that we think they are true makes a powerful illusion that causes our suffering. The Buddha taught that there is no birth, there is no death; there is no coming, there is no going; there is no same, there is no different; there is no permanent self, there is no annihilation. We only think there is. When we understand that we cannot be destroyed, we are liberated from fear. It is a great relief. We can enjoy life and appreciate it in a new way.

Again, I struggle with this concept. It's true that the notion that there is no end and no beginning is a relief to think about. Yet I struggle to remember this idea in my hectic daily life, or when I am

## After This

in the midst of experiencing pain over the loss of something or someone. But again, this is where the Buddhist practice of mindfulness comes into play. Bringing your awareness back to the present moment can be a relief.

In a 2010 interview Oprah Winfrey asked Thich Nhat Hanh what happens when we die. His response reinforces how beneficial the practice of mindfulness can be:

> The question can be answered when you can answer this: What happens in the present moment? In the present moment, you are producing thought, speech, and action. And they continue in the world. Every thought you produce, anything you say, any action you do, it bears your signature. Action is called karma. And that's your continuation. When this body disintegrates, you continue on with your actions. It's like the cloud in the sky. When the cloud is no longer in the sky, it hasn't died. The cloud is continued in other forms like rain or snow or ice. Our nature is the nature of no birth and no death. It is impossible for a cloud to pass from being into nonbeing. And that is true with a beloved person. They have not died. They have continued in many new forms and you can look deeply and recognize them in you and around you.

When I read this interview I immediately thought of my conversations with Rabbi Mendel, and his view that the afterlife is made up of the intentions and actions we take in this lifetime that carry forth in the people around us.

All of these teachings lead me to take a deep breath when my life at large comes swimming up at me. In the moments when I find myself overwhelmed by the path I'm on, by the losses I have incurred, and the deep pain and anguish I am prone to experiencing as a result, I am reminded that letting myself flow deeper into those emotions will not alleviate the pain or the anxiety. I am reminded that the answer to feeling more peaceful is to bring my awareness back to the present moment, to commit to taking actions that honor my intention to live a good life and to make the world a better place, and that by doing so I am honoring my parents and friends who have died, and that as a result, they are still with me.

So I close my eyes and I take a breath. I feel the air passing through my nostrils and I release it. I take another breath.

When I was living in Chicago and working in hospice, I served as not only the bereavement coordinator for our hospice team but also the volunteer coordinator. It was my job to staff the team with people who had offered to volunteer their time to work with the families we served.

The hospice volunteers did a range of things, including grocery errands for family members who were laden with caregiving responsibilities, and even sitting with dying patients who perhaps did not have extended family, or whose caregivers simply needed a break. The volunteers would read to the patients, help them finish tasks, such as writing letters to people they needed to say good-bye to, or just sit with them and talk.

Several times a year I led weekend-long training sessions in which I helped potential volunteers become comfortable with the idea of sitting with a dying person. These training weekends were often intense, as I worked with the volunteers to help them confront their own fears of death, or those fears they held in regard to talking with someone who was facing it.

In the workshop, we did many experiential activities, and one of them in particular proved incredibly effective in allowing people to

## After This

imagine what it might be like to face the end of their lives. In this exercise I asked the group of volunteers to fill out twenty notecards. On each of the first five notecards the volunteers wrote down the names of people or relationships that were dear to them. These could be spouses, children, grandparents, pets—anyone important to them in their life. Each notecard could contain only one name.

On the next five they wrote down five material possessions that were important. These could be anything ranging from a car to a computer to a grandmother's necklace. Again, each notecard contained only one item.

The next five notecards were for hobbies or activities, things such as running, gardening, yoga, writing, taking photographs. And the last five cards were reserved either for places in the volunteer's life that held great meaning or for future events. These could include a summer home they visited often, their garden or swimming pool, or a future date such as a cousin's wedding, a graduation, or an upcoming anniversary.

In the next part of the exercise I asked the volunteers to arrange the cards in order of most important to least important. Usually the first five cards, the ones that contained the people and relationships, came first, and they were followed by a random assortment of the rest. Once the participants had finished arranging their cards, I began to read to them a scenario of an individual who finds out that he or she has become ill with a terminal disease.

At various points over the course of reading through the scenario I would pause and ask the volunteers to give up one or two cards. As the person in the scenario embarked upon various doctor appointments and discovered new information leading to the terminal diagnosis, eventually becoming bedridden and facing the end of his or her life, the volunteers in the group would have to give up card after card. In some cases I would ask them to turn and take a card at random from a tablemate, removing the privilege of the tablemate to pick and choose which important thing he or she would have to relinquish.

The exercise would conclude with the death of the person in the scenario and each volunteer having to give up their final card, this one usually being the most important relationship in their life. Inevitably each person in the group would be in tears, immersed in the experience of what it would be like to let go of everything they once held dear to them.

It was a powerful exercise and one that never failed to remind all of us just how much we hold on to the people and things that we love in our lives, and just how hard it is to give them up.

For the volunteers, it was a helpful experience in allowing them to understand the emotional space they were entering into when sitting down with a dying individual. And for me, it brought me back time and again to the Buddhist notion of desire and attachment.

Before I had begun leading this exercise I had undergone a training session led by another volunteer coordinator, who had used it in the group I was part of. I remember being surprised by how difficult it had actually been for me to give up things like a box of letters from my mother, or my aunt's home on Cape Cod, which I've been visiting since I was a child. As the exercise progressed and my notecards whittled down to the last two, I wept as I gave up my husband, and then my daughter.

When I think back on my experience of this exercise both as a participant and as a workshop instructor, I do not have any comforting answers. To face the end of one's life, or to witness someone else doing so, is deeply painful. There is so much we are forced to let go of in this process. The only ease I have found has been in coming back to the practice of mindfulness, of immersing myself in the present moment, of having the best intentions and making the best choices in the here and now. For the present moment is all that really exists.

## After This

Another tool I used during these trainings was an audio recording by a man named Frank Ostaseski, cofounder of the Zen Hospice Project, in San Francisco. Created in 1987, Zen Hospice was the first Buddhist hospice in America, and it incorporated Buddhist philosophy and teachings into the care of the dying individuals they still serve there today.

In an audio recording titled *Being a Compassionate Companion*, Ostaseski speaks on many different points about what it means to face death, and about caregiving with a compassionate and mindful presence. In every training I held for my volunteers I played several of his tracks.

In one of them Ostaseski says, in his soothing, calm voice, "This is why every spiritual tradition speaks to us of keeping death as our adviser. This is because the recollection of death can lend power, grace, and fullness to every moment of our life, to every action. When we keep death at our fingertips, close at hand, we become less compulsive about gratification. We learn to take ourselves and our ideas a little less seriously. We let go a little more easily."

When I heard these words I always thought of my father's point, that life wouldn't seem as important if there were no death. The fact that there is an end to all of this makes it that much more valuable, just as Ostaseski talks about.

He says, "We understand that even when someone dies, the relationship continues. It's that the person is no longer located outside of us. We are developing what we could call an internal relationship with this person, and that allows us to reinvest in our life. If we follow the path through grief to wholeness, we may discover an undying love."

That's what the afterlife is, I think. At least for those of us who are still living. The afterlife is the relationship we continue to cultivate with our loved ones after they are gone. It is the way we internalize them, the ways in which we continue to bring them into the world, and the way we live in the world in their absence.

---

Five years after using Ostaseski's *Being a Compassionate Companion* audio recording in my hospice volunteer trainings, I travel to San Francisco to visit the actual hospice. The current executive director, a young doctor named BJ Miller, is a triple amputee, having lost both legs and part of one arm in an accident in college.

I wait for BJ in the dining area of the hospice. It's a simple Victorian building in the Mission District, and the room I'm in is sun filled and quiet. There is a bulletin board of photos behind me, depicting patients with their families, and as I look at it I feel a flush of emotion, remembering my time working in hospice and deeply missing it.

I'm musing on my years working with the humor-filled nurses and kindhearted doctors when BJ arrives. Astonishingly handsome, in his early forties, Dr. BJ Miller has an immediately disarming nature about him. He directs me to a living room area, where we sit to talk.

I tell him a bit about my journey, my personal losses, about my grief work in Los Angeles and my time working in hospice in Chicago. I explain that I'm here to speak with him about Buddhism as it relates to the death and dying process, and how a Buddhist perspective might inform our beliefs about the afterlife.

BJ tells me straightaway that he's not a practicing Buddhist. "I can't find any argument with Buddhism," he says. "I'm devoutly agnostic. I love not knowing. I'm perfectly happy with the mystery of it all. The spiritual thing for me is that it's plain as day. It's around us all the time. Death is very matter-of-fact. It's actually quite mundane. The body is this shell. Period. In the moment of death when the body is separated from the spirit, it's incredibly obvious. And that's the profound thing to me. How mundane it is.

## After This

"My spirituality is grounded in that," he continues. "What you can learn in a high school physics class is enough for me to know that we don't know everything, that there are connections among us that are yet discovered. Just that you and I are on the same planet in the same galaxy, in the same time, in the same room . . . to me that alone is amazing enough. I don't need anything more to be really interested in life. And really fascinated with the idea of death," he finishes with a laugh.

I can't help but agree with him. The stark simplicity of death is also what is profound to me about it. I tell BJ about the night my father died, describing what it was like to watch him take his last breaths and then how obvious it was to me in that moment that my father was simply no longer there. His body had become just a body.

In response, BJ recalls his time in the burn unit following his accident. "Yes, you realize that you are not your body. Your body is essential for you to navigate the planet, but there is something about being more than just your flesh. I experienced this sort of knowing, a feeling in myself that I was the same person, even though I was missing some body parts. I had less body, but I was the same person."

I'll find myself musing on this statement of BJ's for weeks after our conversation, trying to imagine what it would be like to lose my own legs, or arms, and knowing that it wouldn't actually change anything about me. It would change my perceptions of the world in some ways, and certainly how the world perceives me, but it wouldn't change the essence of me. I am struck by this. He's right. We are not these bodies.

Our conversation turns to hospice in general. I tell him that one of the components of my work that I was most troubled by was that so often we had patients come to our hospice when they had only days or hours left to live. BJ and I discuss how this issue so often stems from a convergence of several factors, including doctors who are reluctant to give up on their patients, trying treatment after treatment until the very end, along with the patient's and family's own reluctance to give up the medical fight, all blended with a general reluctance to embrace death in our culture as a whole.

"Medical systems are built by default to prop up a body," BJ explains. "Most of us who work within health care understand that it's really flawed. Everything is misaligned. What can you do when you can no longer fix somebody?

"The medical workers are in great moral distress," he continues, "because they know there is a problem that they are complicit in. We as a hospice organization are interested in shifting the culture on this and helping people pay attention to their mortality. The first imperative is to help people turn their attention to it.

"By daring to turn your attention to this subject, and daring to confront your own mortality, much more often than not, most people report back that there's this great pot of gold at the end of that rainbow. They report that they feel much more engaged with their life, they appreciate their time while they have it, and they make decisions differently being aware of the finiteness of their bodily life. So we're also aware, as is anyone who works in hospice, that there's this beauty waiting for people when they do welcome it.

"The big thing is how do you help people pay attention to something that's very hard to pay attention to? I think denial is part of it. But my experience is that it's gone from frank denial to, 'Okay, I get that we all die, but how do I deal with it?' It comes around to the *how*."

"Yes," I agree. "It's one thing to accept that you're dying, but there are still a great many fears around that. Hospice provides a community that will support you in the experience, people who will take care of you as you die."

BJ agrees, but he thinks that not enough people realize this. He

## After This

tells me that at the UCSF Medical Center, at the University of California, San Francisco, where he is a palliative care doctor, "hospice numbers are down, and there are more ICU deaths. People are electing, even when palliative care gets involved, for much more aggressive treatment. I've really been shocked to see this shift. I'm really concerned about some of the numbers. I mean, forty-two percent of Californians died in hospice in 2012. That's almost half. But fully a third of those were on hospice for less than a week."

What he's describing is exactly what I saw in my hospice in Chicago, with the way patients would come on with only a day or two to live.

"Here it's like a salvage job," BJ says. "In a day or two, maybe we can get a little physical comfort for the patient, make a little space to dwell in the emotional realm, maybe have a reconciling conversation or two, and maybe eke out a salvaged, non-horrible death. That's better than the alternative. The final imagery here is very different than all the tubes and whatnot in a hospital. And therefore I think people are set up to grieve differently here.

"I guess the goal, really, is pushing that experience a little bit farther upstream. If you can eke it out in the last day or so, why not two weeks, why not a month? And then maybe we can start having these conversations before you're even diagnosed with something. Why wait to be dying to have palliative care? Why even wait until you're sick to have these conversations?

"Because the thing is, there's a pathway to life enhancement that comes with thinking about death. My job is to inform you, as the palliative care doctor, about all of your options. Some people, even when their eyes are wide open, still want to go down swinging. Okay, and I will help support that. But most people, if they understand all their options, they elect a different way."

I tell BJ about the differences between my parents' deaths. My mother was one of the ones who went down swinging. Even after her oncology doctors told her that there was nothing more they could do for her, and had recommended hospice, she went on to find a hospital that was willing to conduct a few experimental treatments. When she finally died, it was in a hospital following a round of brutal surgeries and treatments that had debilitated her further. There had been no time allowed for any of us to have conversations about the end of her life, or for us to say good-bye to each other.

My father's death was quite different. Although the doctors had offered to keep trying to treat his cancer with various methods, he knew that he was facing the end of his life, and he elected to go home under the care of hospice. We had several weeks together in which my father rested comfortably, and during that time we were able to review his life together, and to say good-bye.

"I think deaths that go poorly are horrible and horrifying and so tough, and there are a lot of lessons in there," BJ says. "Some of my best teaching has been being involved in deaths that don't go well. We need to reveal some of those regrets and also highlight when things can go so beautifully as well."

"Yes," I tell him. "My father's death was beautiful. It was what death should be. He was at home and comfortable and he had the chance to find peace with the end of his life."

"A lot of us would like to die at home," BJ replies. "And more and more we're dying in slower, more protracted ways with multiple illnesses that have been managed, but that lead to these protracted dying phases. We have family members who can't take time off. So it's getting harder and harder to die well, at home. But places like Zen Hospice make that possible.

"We need to build more structures like this. It's outside the system, though. Insurance doesn't fund this. We need to build structures to house these experiences, to make them real, to witness them.

## After This

Our volunteers go back in the world and talk about the beautiful deaths that happened here."

I lean back in my chair, buzzing from our conversation. I intended to talk about Buddhism and the philosophy of dying, but what BJ and I are touching on suddenly seems so much more important. And I realize that it flows into the Buddhist teachings after all. What we are talking about is being present to death, and fully allowing it to be a part of our lives.

So much of the work I did in hospice involved helping clients come to terms with the fact that they did not face their loved one's death in the last days. They told me that they were still holding out hope that this one last treatment or one last surgery would work, that they would have more time with this person. They told me all the things they wished they could have done or said if they had truly understood that this was the end.

People mistakenly think that hospice is a death sentence, but that doesn't have to be true. In my hospice in Chicago we had some patients who were with us for close to two years, and we even had some patients who had their hospice services revoked because they began to get better and were no longer facing a terminal diagnosis. The flux of care surrounding a person in hospice can be so great that the medical stress they were under often disappears, allowing them to feel better and sometimes even heal. But because our culture is so fearful of dying, hospice is so often viewed as the last nail in the coffin.

This doesn't have to be the case. What BJ said about starting to have these conversations about dying earlier in our lives is key. I am certain that were we to have more frank discussions with our loved ones about our eventual deaths, there would be less confusion and remorse when they actually occur.

On my drive home to Los Angeles, I go over and over our

conversation in my head. BJ's statement about the awareness he felt following his accident that he was not his body runs through my mind continually.

We are not these bodies. But accepting that fact while we are still in them is the hard part.

---

One night while I am brushing my teeth, I recall a mindfulness technique I read about once that centers on focusing your attention on mundane tasks that we normally do not pay attention to. Brushing your teeth was one of the examples mentioned. The literature suggested that rather than spacing out as you brush your teeth—a time when we normally allow our thoughts to wander to tasks we will be faced with the next day, or things we need to take care of before we go to bed—spend the time really focusing on the task itself. In doing so, in concentrating on the feeling of the bristles against your gums, on the way the toothbrush feels in your hand, on the way the toothpaste tastes in your mouth, you are bringing your awareness to the present moment, rather than dwelling on the past or future.

That night, lying in bed with the girls, I try to teach them in a roundabout way how to be present. After we are done reading books and talking about school the next day, I ask them to lie still beside me and think about the way their bodies feel.

"Think about your feet right now and how the sheets feel on them," I say. "Let your legs relax. Feel your tummy get soft and your shoulders relax."

I can feel them squirm a bit next to me as they bring their attention to their bodies, but then slowly each of the girls grows still.

"Can you feel yourself breathing?" I ask.

"Yes, Mama," Vera answers softly.

"Isn't it cool that even when you fall asleep, your body just keeps

## After This

breathing?" I ask her. Jules puts a hand on my arm, and I concentrate on the heat flowing between our skin.

"How does it know how to do that?" Vera asks.

"That's how our bodies work," I tell her. "They don't always need us to be telling them what to do."

"But I can take a deep breath if I want to," Vera says, puffing out some big exhalations.

"Yes, absolutely," I say. "Our bodies are like houses that we live in. We're connected to them in very important ways. Like how tears come out of our eyes if we get sad. But they are not all that we are."

Vera keeps taking deep breaths for a while, and I can feel Juliette falling asleep next to me, her own breathing growing slow and steady, her body growing still. Vera reaches around in the dark until she finds my hand, gripping it tightly.

"I love you, Mama," she whispers.

"I love you more," I whisper back.

"I love you to the moon and back," she says, something we've taken to saying to each other frequently.

"I love you as big as the universe," I respond.

"I love you even bigger than the universe," she says, and I can hear the smile in her voice.

"Always," I say. "We'll always love each other that much, even when we're not in these bodies anymore."

"Always," she whispers.

I can feel her body soften after that, and I listen to her breathing grow slow and steady like her sister's. They're both asleep now and I lie there in the dark for a while, each of them curled into me.

Even if we are not these bodies, we are these bodies right now. I let myself grow mindful of this very moment, the feeling of my own body, and of theirs, warm and flush against me. There is no past, no future. There is only this moment.

# Claire Bidwell Smith

Dear Vera and Jules,

When I was in fourth grade my beloved golden retriever, Annie, died. We had just moved to a small town in Florida and everything was new. Had it not been for Annie I would have felt terribly lonely. She was a loyal dog, and we spent our afternoons when I returned from school wading through the bay in front of our house and taking long walks through the woods.

Annie was truly my best friend. I told her all my secrets, pouring my heart out to her at night before I fell asleep as she lay at the foot of my bed. And then one afternoon I returned home from shopping with my father. I mistakenly left the car door open in the driveway and before I went to my room for a nap my dad spied the open door through the window and reminded me to close it.

I wandered outside into the hot Florida sun and slammed shut the door, not realizing that Annie had jumped into the backseat while the door was still open. I went inside and took a nap and when I woke up a couple of hours later I went on a hunt to find my sweet dog. I looked everywhere, and finally spied a glimpse of her fur through the windshield of my father's car. I ran to the car, excited to have finally found her, but when I opened the door I realized that she was dead.

It was a horrific accident, one that cut through me deeply for many years. Our little family grieved. My mother wept for weeks, not just for the loss of Annie, but

## After This

because I had to experience such pain and remorse. Annie was cremated and for almost a year I slept with her ashes in an urn on my nightstand.

One day when my parents were out, I took the urn and I waded out in the warm, shallow bay in front of our house. It was a place where Annie and I had spent a lot of time together, walking through the knee-high water, chasing horseshoe crabs and overturning rocks to peer at little sea creatures.

That day I walked far out into the water, tears dripping down my cheeks, and I opened the urn and scattered Annie's ashes into the water around me. I told her how sorry I was, how much I loved her, and how much I would always miss her. Remembering this moment still brings tears to my eyes, almost thirty years later.

I'm telling you this story because I know now that Annie never doubted how much I loved her, that in whatever way she was capable of, she knew that I never intended to hurt her. I'm telling you this story because if ever I die suddenly, I want you to know that there is nothing you could be left wanting to say to me that I wouldn't already know.

I know with every ounce of my being how much you love me. No matter what lies ahead, there is nothing you could ever do that would make me doubt your love. No fight, no lie, no transgression, no sharp words spoken could ever change my love for you, or the fact that I know you love me.

For years after my mother died I regretted my tumultuous teenage years with her. I felt deep remorse for the fights we'd had or the awful things I'd said to her now and again. I hated myself for not being there the night she died, for not telling her one last time how much I loved her.

And then you girls were born, and I realized in an instant that she had known. That she'd always known how much I loved her, that she knew how much I would miss her and how grateful I was for her.

And so too, I know this about both of you.

Rest easy with any distance that comes our way. Know that there will never be anything outstanding between us. I have written you all these letters, told you so very many things that I've wished to convey, but you girls have written me your own letters. You've traced your love for me in a thousand kisses and snuggles and tears and moments. You've told me the stories of who you are, you've shown me your futures, you've split yourselves wide open in the face of your love for me.

And nothing will ever erase that.

Forever in love with you,

*Mama*

# Chapter Seven

I'm standing at a podium, in front of a room full of eighty women who have all lost their mothers. It's a Saturday in Los Angeles and I'm one of the presenters at author Hope Edelman's first annual Motherless Daughters Conference.

I take a breath, watching the women in the room get settled in their chairs. They range in age from eighteen to sixty-five, and I know that if anyone else were to walk into this room right now they'd simply see of an assortment of various women seated together. But I know that what we all have in common runs so deep that despite our ages and backgrounds, we are more alike than not.

This tribe of women is one I never, ever wanted to be part of, and in a thousand ways I wish I weren't here. I wish none of us were here. We should be rushing about our busy lives, meeting our mothers for lunch or chatting with them on the phone while we change diapers, filling them in on the latest achievement of our growing families. We should be settled in our lives, fulfilled and engaged and connected.

But we're not. We are here because something is missing. Our mothers have died, and as a result we have lost a piece of ourselves.

I continue to watch them get settled and I am struck by how at home I feel with these women, not having spoken to a single one of them. They understand me in a way that most people do not. The feeling I have right now is the same one I had the first time I saw Hope Edelman's book *Motherless Daughters*.

It was 1998 and I was living in New York. My mother had been gone for a year and a half and I was floundering in my existence without her. I was in college and waiting tables and I was utterly lost. I felt completely alone in my grief; it seemed that the whole world was carrying on around me while I struggled to get out of bed in the morning.

One afternoon on my way home from work I stopped at the bookstore. As I was browsing the shelves I came across Hope's book. The words *motherless daughter* jumped out at me and I stopped and stood there, just staring. The feeling was the same one I have right now as I look at these women. All I could think, for the first time since my mother had died, was *I am not alone*.

It was a profound moment for me, one in which I realized that there were other women out there just like me, working to understand themselves in the face of their mothers' absence. The fact that there was an entire book dedicated to the subject was a revelation to me. Not only did it tell me that I wasn't alone, but it gave validity to my deep feelings of pain and confusion. Staring at Hope's book, I understood that losing a mother was a terrible thing to experience, and when I read the pages it contained I understood even more about why it was so hard.

Finally the conference room has quieted and it's time for me to begin. Hope has asked me to present a lecture on how connecting with the afterlife can have a healing impact on our grief process, and I've thought long and hard about what I want to impart to these women. I begin by telling them the story of losing my own mother, about the day I saw Hope's book on the shelf, and my quest over the

## After This

past several years to find a way back to my mother. I describe the impact that becoming a mother has had on me, and how it has driven me to search for a better understanding of how we stay connected to those we lose, even in death.

I tell them a bit about the mediums I've seen, about my talks with the rabbi, and my past-life regressions. I can tell that they are interested and engaged. They too are desperate to retain a connection with their own mothers. But in relating all the experiences I've had researching this book, the one I most want to tell them about is my foray into shamanism.

---

Almost a year ago I spent a month engrossed in two intensive shamanic workshops put on by the Foundation for Shamanic Studies. I traveled to Phoenix, Arizona, and Bozeman, Montana, in order to attend these workshops, and the revelations that came forth were profound ones for me.

Shamanism is an ethereal practice, but one that I'd been hearing about for years. When I first moved to Los Angeles it quickly became apparent that I had entered into a world rich with new age spirituality. I lived in Venice Beach and the friends I made were artistic and eclectic. They went to Burning Man every year, taking hallucinogens and camping out under the stars; they held mother-blessing rituals instead of traditional baby showers; they saw therapists and acupuncturists regularly; and they went to shamanic healers instead of medical doctors.

Initially I scoffed at these endeavors. I refused to go to Burning Man, showed up reluctantly at the mother blessings clutching some kind of moonstone I'd been instructed to bring along, and raised my eyebrows at the tales of shamanic healing. It all just seemed too far out.

## Claire Bidwell Smith

Years later, as I began to delve into my afterlife research and let myself grow comfortable with the past-life regressions, the astrology, and the psychic mediums, I found myself wondering again about shamanism. One night a cursory Internet search led me to the website for the Foundation of Shamanic Studies and this course description:

> Michael Harner's Shamanism, Dying, and Beyond
>
> Participants learn how to deal with the issue of dying and the destiny of souls from a shamanic perspective. The workshop is both for those who wish to learn for themselves, and for those who wish to help others who are in terminal situations or who have already passed on. Experiences to be undertaken include learning how to become experientially familiar with the after-death realms, tracking a person using shamanic journeying, completing unfinished business, helping a person to cross over, and classic psychopomp work.

The more I read, the more interested I became. The tenets of shamanism center heavily around practitioners taking spiritual journeys through their consciousness in order to understand their lives and the world around them on a deeper level. Although it sounded heady, I grew more and more curious about it, especially if it could lead me to a deeper understanding of the afterlife. I'd also heard of many therapists in Los Angeles who used shamanic work to help aid in their clients' journeys of self-exploration.

I signed up for the shaman course and two weeks later I was standing in an overly air-conditioned hotel conference room in Phoenix, holding a green plastic baby rattle that I'd stolen from Vera's bedroom, ready to partake in my first soul dance.

## After This

It all seemed ridiculous from the get-go, accessing various spiritual realms through the use of drumming and dancing. I couldn't think of anything more outside my comfort zone. But after opening myself up to all the rest of the kooky things I'd done in the previous year, I felt willing to give this one a try.

I spent that first workshop in Phoenix—an introductory course in shamanism—learning how to lie back on a yoga mat with a mask over my eyes, taking dreamlike journeys to meet my spirit animals, all to the insistent beat of a drum. Friends back in L.A. had offered to introduce me to shamans in Malibu or Topanga who used the hallucinogenic ayahuasca plant from South America to induce similar kinds of journeys, but with two small children at home, my experimental drug forays have officially come to a close.

I'm grateful that not all shamans use ayahuasca; others opt to use the more traditional drumming, one that stimulates theta waves in the brain, promoting a dreamlike state that encourages the "journeys" you take in your mind. I work to explain all this to the women at the Motherless Daughters Conference, and they laugh along with me as I describe my reluctance to buy one of those big hippie drums and don a serape for the workshops, instead showing up in jeans and flats, Vera's green plastic baby rattle clutched in my hand.

I immediately found the shamanic journeys I took similar to the experiences I had with past-life regression. Both are about letting your mind grow so relaxed that you are able to open up to the various images and stories that flow forth. In that first workshop in Phoenix I journeyed to both the "upper world" and the "lower world," both being realms that shamans believe exist outside this one, and I met my first spirit animal, which turned out to be a great white shark. I didn't really believe that I was traveling to these realms, communing with sharks and whatnot, but I did enjoy the practice of letting my mind create these stories, and I dissected them as a therapist would, attributing meaning and symbolism to the things I conjured up.

In the grief work I've done with clients, I've spent a lot of time thinking about the various stories we tell ourselves about our lives and our losses. As a writer it has come naturally to me to explore narratives, and what I've found in the work I've done is that by examining these narratives we can find ways to change them. We can recognize that the stories we tell ourselves about our lives are exactly that: stories. We can change the stories, edit them, rewrite them, look at them through a different lens. And sometimes the stories we carry around about ourselves are buried so deeply in our subconscious that we need help in order to see them.

That's exactly what the shamanic journeys provided for me—another way to explore the ways I've internalized the events that have shaped my life.

And so it was during my experience at the Bozeman workshop that I came to understand something very important about my story, about my mother's death. And this is what I most want to impart to the women at the Motherless Daughters Conference.

I liked being in Bozeman that weekend, away from Los Angeles and my children and my hectic life for a couple of days. I checked into a spooky old bed-and-breakfast on the edge of town, and I showed up for my workshop each morning, Vera's green plastic baby rattle and my notebook tucked away in my bag.

The instructors were a man and woman named David Corbin and Nan Moss, both of them seasoned teachers in the world of shamanism. They were each in their sixties, and instead of looking

## After This

supremely hippieish, as I had anticipated, they both just looked like nature lovers: hiking boots, suede vests, some Navajo jewelry.

The group of participants was a large one, twenty-five in attendance, and at least half of them belonged to an actual shaman's circle based in Bozeman. I sat on a pillow in the corner and took slow, steady breaths, enjoying the time to get centered.

Everything about the shamanic practice was so noticeably different from my busy day-to-day life in Los Angeles, driving my children around to school and various extracurricular activities, seeing clients, making a thousand stops at the grocery store, and immersing myself in a constant stream of media that ran the gamut from Instagram to HBO. If I was lucky, I got to a yoga class once a week, and at least once a day I lamented the fact that my meditation practice was at an all-time low. The saturated time of meditation and reflection during these workshops felt good.

The Bozeman workshop was held in a dance studio in an old creative arts building. Oak trees whispered outside the open windows and the wood floor creaked beneath my feet. Something about the room felt familiar and conjured up childhood nostalgia. Nan and David took turns talking about death and dying in the context of shamanism and I listened intently.

According to shamanic beliefs, the soul migrates to one of the three spiritual worlds after death. Most often, it arrives in the middle world, and from there it goes on to do work, usually in the upper world. Souls who are confused or stuck, or still attached somehow to this realm, remain in the middle world, hence the reason for its murkiness.

According to Nan and David, many of the souls are trapped there out of guilt or fear or because they have been unable to let go of a person or a belief they carried during life. Nan gave examples that included people who had committed suicide or harmed others.

She explained that when the souls of these kinds of people migrate after death there tends to be much confusion and remorse. They wander the middle world, trying to make sense of where to go next. Sometimes they are not even aware that they are dead, she told us.

For our first journey that weekend Nan and David instructed us to travel to the lower world and meet with an animal who would become our guide to the afterlife. I laughed a bit in my head, thinking about how comfortable I've become with ideas like spirit animals, and then I lay back on my mat preparing for the journey. Months later, standing before the women at the Motherless Daughters Conference, I find it difficult to describe these journeys and how they work, but I remind myself that the nuances aren't as important as the underlying messages I discovered.

In that first journey in Bozeman a large brown bear appeared to me in my vision and I followed him into the woods until we came to an old stone cottage. It was a simple, one-room structure, and I followed the bear inside. The room was bare except for a figure in one corner, and as I drew closer I saw that she was a young woman, and she was sitting in a corner with her knees pulled to her chest. She was a transparent gray color, and immobile. Everything about her emanated a profound sadness.

I approached the girl and touched her gently on the shoulder, but she didn't respond.

"Don't worry about her right now," the bear told me, and so I didn't, although the sad gray figure stayed with me.

After each journey in the workshop we would sit around in a circle and share our experiences. I listened to the other practitioners describe the animals they'd met with and the things they'd seen along the way. I declined to share about my bear and the gray girl, not sure what it all meant just yet.

After lunch that day Nan and David gave us a lecture on the

## After This

concept of "dismembering." The philosophy of dismemberment is that if you dismember the physical body you are able to release unhealthy attachments, and you can remember your true spiritual self. Dismemberment also allows you to release a hold that you may have on limitations such as illness, grief, unhealthy relationships, or something that seems impossible to change. Nan and David warned that there can be sadness and pain in the dismemberment process, but that ultimately great healing can come from it.

This made sense to me in many ways, reminding me of thoughts about the narratives we tell ourselves. I am constantly working with clients to help them release or reconsider long-held beliefs about themselves or others. It's almost always apparent that those very beliefs have served the purpose of avoiding the pain of change, of facing truth or admitting failure. I have long believed that we hold on to grief as a way of staying connected to our lost loved ones.

A client of mine who lost her husband internalized the idea that she simply wasn't good enough to have a husband in the first place, and that perhaps he wouldn't have died had she been a better wife. Together we worked through those feelings, and I've tried to help her separate the real story of her husband's sudden death from her feelings of abandonment and unworthiness. I'm constantly amazed by how insidious grief can be, snaking its way into even our self-esteem.

As we prepared for our own journeys of dismemberment that afternoon, I was not thinking very much of my own attachments, of what I might be holding on to, but I felt cautious all the same. In the journey we were to ask our animal to dismember us, and as the drums began, I followed my bear into a wooded glade, where we stood inside a circle of trees. It was a beautiful forest, green and magical, and I stared at the large bear before me and quietly asked him to dismember me.

Without hesitation and in several quick strokes, the bear ripped me limb from limb. It was a painless experience, but startling nonetheless. My spirit, or my soul, or whatever part of me exists outside of my physical form, immediately sprang up into the trees around me. I was not just one particular tree, but all of them. I was there, part of the forest, and I was gazing down at the remnants of Claire Bidwell Smith.

The experience was unlike any I had ever had. There was a deft and certain knowledge that I was not my body. I was not my physical form. I was, in fact, much more than that. It was the kind of knowingness that Dr. BJ Miller, at the Zen Hospice Project, had referenced when speaking of a similar awareness he experienced after losing his limbs. It was the same kind of knowingness I had felt when looking at my father's body after he died.

I stared down at the broken-apart pieces of Claire Bidwell Smith, taking in the sight of her legs still encased in her mint green jeans, her head and arms all in different places, and with that came an utter faith in the truth that this woman is not all that I am. Then I was flooded with the most profound feeling of relief.

I'm not sure how long this vision went on for, but soon I was called back to the room, and I sat up out of my trance, tears immediately flowing down my cheeks as I felt a deep disappointment to be back in my physical form, back in the body of Claire Bidwell Smith. I pulled out my notebook and attempted to write down my experience, but the tears would not stop, my throat was closing up, and finally I pushed my way to standing and exited the room.

I walked down the hallway of the art center, the floor creaking beneath me, until I found a stairwell, and I sat perched on one of the steps, trying to stifle my sobs with the sleeve of my shirt. The stairwell brought back a memory of sitting in just such a place at the hospital where I last saw my mother, another time when I hid away to cry in private.

## After This

I looked down at the teardrops on my jeans and I didn't want to be there; I didn't want to be in that body again. I didn't want to be Claire Bidwell Smith, and everything that came with her. The confusion of marriage and motherhood that I was experiencing, the grief and loss of my parents that had followed me into adulthood, the new persona as an author that I had taken on. It all felt heavy and cloying and complicated compared to my experience as part of the trees in the forest.

I have read countless stories of people who have had out-of-body experiences. Some of them came from deep meditation practices, some of them from near-death accidents. In all of them the author recounted the feeling of bliss and freedom, the comfort in knowing that we are not just these physical forms. My thoughts turned to a friend of mine in Los Angeles, a young mother like me, who had breast cancer and was terrified of the war raging inside her body. I wished for her that she could experience this same relief I had felt so briefly, this strange certainty that there is more to us than these bodies.

The vision, the journey, or whatever it was had been utterly overwhelming. It wasn't that I had never thought of myself as something other than this person I had always been, but I had never *felt* it. And in the wake of that feeling everything about the person I was seemed constructed and unnecessary. I felt a deep sadness that she was someone I didn't necessarily want to be, but also a release in the idea that I didn't have to be her either, that all the things I thought made up who I was were not important, that there was something more to me.

When I finally pulled myself together enough to reenter the room, I listened with interest to the experiences that others in the group had had. I was not the only one who'd felt such a profound release, and I shared my vision with the group. Nan nodded at me, as though she was proud of me, but then she paused.

"Were you re-membered at the end of the experience?" she asked.

I shook my head no, recalling that we had been instructed to ask our animal to "re-member" us at the end of the journey. I also realized that even had I remembered to do this, I'm not sure I would have.

"Hmmm," Nan said. "That means there is more work ahead. Not a bad thing, but something to pay attention to."

On the last day of the workshop I woke up at five a.m., determined to take in some more of this beautiful part of the country before I had to head back to Los Angeles. I got in my rental car, knowing I didn't have to be at the workshop until nine a.m., and I drove an hour away to Gallatin National Forest. I watched the sun rise over the valley and I drove by a lake so still it didn't look real. It was just past six a.m. when I parked my car at the entrance to the hiking trail. There were no other cars in the lot and it was so cold that I could see my breath.

I pulled my hoodie tighter around me and set off toward the trailhead. There was a map at the entrance and I checked it against the directions I had. There was a waterfall I wanted to try to reach, and I studied the map, making sure I knew where I was going. Just before I turned toward the trailhead I noticed a sign next to the map. It read:

**BEAR COUNTRY**
**Do not travel alone.**
**Do not approach bears.**
**Carry bear spray.**

I read this sign several times, realizing that I was very much alone, and that I did not have bear spray. I paused, looking down the winding trail before me, at the morning sunlight just beginning to filter through the trees, and I debated whether I should proceed. All

## After This

my old death anxiety flared up. I thought of my girls back at home, of my whole little life, about what would happen if I died.

And then my vision from yesterday swam back to me, my scattered limbs on the forest floor from the bear's blows, and instantly a feeling of peace replaced the anxiety. I began to walk, and with each step I took along the trail I realized that I was no longer fearing death as much as I once did. I perked up with each rustle I heard in the forest, wondering if, at any moment, a bear would step out of the woods, but I was not afraid. If I was to be torn limb from limb, so be it.

All those years of being afraid to leave behind the people I loved, of relinquishing the things I wanted to accomplish in this lifetime. I had been afraid of what lies beyond this world, this life. But right then, walking that path through the forest, I only felt peaceful. It wasn't that I wished to die—far from it—only that, after my dismemberment experience, death didn't seem as final as it once had.

I made it all the way to the waterfall without encountering any bears. The forest had come alive along the way, birds chirping and rabbits hopping across my path. I stood before the cascading falls and took a moment to feel grateful for that moment in my life. I still wasn't sure what the answer to any of this was, still didn't know what happens when we die, but I did know that it felt good to be asking those questions, to be opening myself up to the possibility of something more.

I made it back to the workshop on time and settled in for our first journey of the day. Nan went through the ritual of lighting a candle, offering up tiny leaves of tobacco and incense to the spirits. She walked around the little altar she had made in the center of the room, shaking her rattle and calling out an eerie whistling. When she announced that before our journey we were going to do a power animal dance, I didn't even balk; I just stood up holding my green plastic rattle.

## Claire Bidwell Smith

As a group, we began to move around the room in a circle, letting our animals flow through us. People were suddenly crawling on all fours, some were hooting or cawing, others were baying like coyotes at the dance room ceiling. I closed my eyes, trying to hide the smile on my face and feeling grateful that I could just do some silent gliding on behalf of my great white shark.

Months later when I'm describing this image to the room of motherless daughters I cannot help but laugh, and they are laughing too. There is a poignancy to it, a knowing even as I recount this story that I have been driven to these absurd moments all from a place of deep grief over the loss of my mother.

When the dance concluded we took our places on the floor with blankets and pillows, preparing for another journey. This time we were instructed to travel with our animal to the middle world, where we would ask to speak with someone who was deceased. I slipped my eye mask on and settled into the sound of the drums, dropping down into the murkiness until I was there with my bear. Although it was my mother whom I most wanted to see, I was hesitant to ask about her. Instead I asked to speak with Julie.

Images came and went and Julie arrived, but her presence didn't feel authentic, more like I was actively conjuring her from my imagination, rather than the way many of these visions had felt. During my journeys so far I had worked hard to keep my conscious imagination out of it, trying instead to be open to the images that naturally flowed forth, resisting the impulse to produce them. And in that case, standing before my dead friend, it felt forced, as though I were pulling up old memories or images from photographs. I tried to let go, but nothing more came.

Finally, I relented and asked the bear if I could see my mother. He nodded and began to amble forth. The images were flowing again finally and I did not feel as though I had a direct hand in producing

## After This

them. I followed the bear through the forest and back to the same stone cottage I had visited the day before, when I first met the bear. We walked inside and the gray girl was still there in the corner, motionless, knees pulled to her chest.

The bear nodded in her direction, speaking to me. "That is a piece of your soul that your mother took with her when she died. She comes here to tend it. We can wait for her."

I stood agape, staring at the figure in the corner, trying to process what the bear had just said. Eventually I turned back to look at the open door of the cottage, hoping to see my mother, but she did not come. Finally the sound of the drums signaled the end of the journey, and reluctantly I left the cottage, traveling back to ordinary reality.

When I tell this part of the story to the motherless daughters I reiterate the same revelation I'd had when I first experienced the journey. "When the people we love die, when our mothers die," I tell them, "we lose a piece of ourselves. It's that simple."

I look around at their faces, all these women, and I see tears in their eyes, muffled crying, and nods from all around the room. "We try so hard," I tell them, "to make this not be true. But we can't. Part of us is gone, and we are forever changed."

After I had come out of the journey in which the bear finally explained who the gray girl was, I jotted down my thoughts in my notebook, and then waited eagerly for the rest of the class to finish so that we could begin to share. I wanted to tell Nan and David about the gray girl and what the bear had said about her being part of my soul. As I waited, the memory of a dream came to me from years ago, shortly after I lost my mother.

In the dream I was sitting at a large dining room table with my extended family for Thanksgiving dinner. It was a pleasant scene. I was sitting next to my father, who was still living at the time of the dream, and all my cousins and aunts and uncles were present. We were just about to begin our feast when I noticed that my mother was on the floor next to my chair. She was weeping and begging for me to leave the table and join her. In the dream I felt incredibly conflicted about stepping away from my family and the meal we were about to have, but I also could not bear to leave my mother by herself there on the floor. I had awoken before I had to make a decision, and had immediately begun to sob.

Everything about the idea of part of my soul having gone with my mother—our unwillingness to let go of each other, like the myth of Persephone, in which the daughter is allowed to leave the underworld for part of the year to be with her mother—reminded me of this dream.

Finally in the workshop everyone was ready to begin talking about their journeys, and I raised my hand eagerly. I hadn't shared much in this workshop yet, and I could tell that people perked up with interest. I told the group first about my initial meeting with the bear and how we had visited the cottage where I had seen the gray girl in the corner. Then I recounted how we had gone back to that place today, and what the bear had said about my mother.

Nan and David nodded, as though this made sense to them.

"Did the bear say that your mother 'took' part of your soul with her, or that you 'sent' part of your soul with her?" Nan asked.

I reviewed the memory and answered her. "He definitely said that she 'took' part of it."

Nan nodded again. "This is common," she said, looking around the room and addressing all of us. "Often when we lose someone, or when we simply go through a traumatic experience, we lose little pieces of our soul. One of the services many shamans perform is called a soul retrieval. This is when a shaman takes a journey in order to retrieve the pieces of your soul that get lost like this."

## After This

Nan began to tell me about a shaman she knew of in Los Angeles who could do just such a retrieval for me, but she was cut off by a young Native American participant sitting directly across from me.

"I'm sorry," he said, "but I just can't wait to share any longer. Something happened in my journey that relates directly to Claire's experience."

I turned away from Nan, curious to hear what this man had to say. During this workshop, and the one in Phoenix, there were several instances in which people had experienced similar journeys, or had seen things in their own journeys that someone else in the room had also seen.

"In my journey," he said, "I asked my power animal, who also happens to be a bear, to take me to see my cousin who died. In the journey we went into an old house in the woods—it wasn't a cottage, exactly, because it had different rooms and levels—but on the ground floor, in the first room we went into, there was a gray figure sitting in a corner. When I got closer I realized it was a girl."

At this point, the man described how she was sitting with her knees pulled to her chest, a detail I hadn't shared with the room.

"She was all kind of translucent, just like Claire described. I asked my bear if this was my cousin, and he replied no, that she was for someone else, and he directed me to another portion of the house."

Chills ran up and down my limbs, and I could feel everyone in the room watching me and the man across from me as we connected over this experience.

"Very cool," David said, and again Nan nodded, as though both of them had heard of this kind of thing before.

In that moment, it all seemed real—the connections we all shared, the energy in that room, the idea of there being much more to reality than we can possibly conceive. And although I felt perplexed by the myriad questions running through my mind, I also felt that same strange peacefulness I'd felt in the forest that morning, the sense that we humans are much more than we give ourselves credit for.

And all those months later, standing before the motherless daughters as they weep and acknowledge that they too have lost a piece of their own souls, I can feel nothing but awe for the deep ways in which we love and lose each other in these lifetimes.

For weeks after the Bozeman workshop I couldn't stop thinking about the gray girl in the cottage. My heart broke at the thought of my mother holding on to me in that way, and also at the idea that part of me was possibly missing.

Back in Los Angeles my life resumed at full speed. It was jolting to go from the days of meditative journeys back into my hectic schedule of work and kids and errands, but there was also some relief in it. This was the world I lived in, not one of forests and wooded cottages, of mystical animals and ritual. But all the same, there were elements of that realm I wanted to incorporate into my daily life, a certain reverence for our deeper selves that I wanted to honor.

At the airport I had purchased a tiny figurine of a bear, and two stuffed bears for my girls, and back at home I placed the figurine next to a few rocks I had collected in Sedona during my past-life research. The sight of it nagged at me in the mornings when I woke up, and a week after the workshop I placed a call to the shaman Nan had told me about, a woman named Amanda Foulger.

Amanda lives in Topanga Canyon, a community in the mountains north of Santa Monica, known for its hippie philosophy and new age spiritualism. I told Amanda a little about the workshop in Bozeman and how Nan had suggested I visit her for a soul retrieval. We made an appointment and a couple of weeks later I found myself driving the winding canyon road on my way to her house.

## After This

I parked my car in the sloped driveway. Amanda's house is perched on the edge of the mountain, lush trees and plants cascading down from every direction. Just before I rang the doorbell, I noticed a statue of a bear by the front mat. Amanda, in her sixties, with gray hair and a charming gap between her teeth, greeted me warmly. She welcomed me into her living room and I took a look around before sitting down on a nearby futon. Incense was burning and candles were lit in a cluster by one of the windows. There were crystal balls and dream catchers, and there were also bear figurines everywhere.

Amanda sat across from me and I told her a little about my life, about the loss of my parents, and specifically about my mother's death. I recounted my journeys in Bozeman with the bear and I told her what he had told me about the gray girl in the corner. She nodded, as Nan had done, and agreed that a soul retrieval was in order.

She instructed me to lie back on the futon and gave me a mask to place over my eyes. She told me that she was going to journey on my behalf and do her best to work with my experience. She said that my only job was to relax as much as possible and try to remain in an open, meditative state. I took a few deep breaths and tried to clear my thoughts. Above me Amanda began to do that same eerie whistling Nan had done in our workshop, and she shook a rattle loudly over and across me, the sound entrancing.

I'm not sure how much time went by—twenty minutes, perhaps thirty—but finally Amanda called me out of my state. I removed the mask and opened my eyes. She was sitting across from me and there were tears in her eyes.

"I made an enormous amount of progress," she told me. "Oh, your mother loves you so, so much."

A lump formed in my throat and I could feel tears in my eyes.

"I went to the stone cottage," she said. "And your mother was there. She was so tired. She felt so responsible for you, so unable to let go of you. She had been so worried about you and she just didn't know how to let go. She hadn't been ready to die."

Tears were dripping down my cheeks.

"She was so attached to you that she didn't even know that she was supposed to move on. She didn't realize that there was more to the afterlife, that she has other work she is supposed to be doing. Both of you have been holding on to each other across the realms, but it's been holding both of you back from the real work you are both supposed to be doing, in this world and that one," Amanda said, her voice soft and gentle.

"I called in your father, and he helped me to guide her away. I reminded her that she would still be able to check in on you, but that she needed to let go of this part of you she's been holding on to."

I took a deep breath. Part of me wanted to ask Amanda to go back, to take it all back. I didn't want my mother to let go of me—not now, not there, or here, or ever. But I also knew she was right, that my grief and longing for my mother had prevented me from moving on in my life in many ways. So I just nodded at Amanda, and let the tears fall into my lap.

"Claire," she said, "your soul is ready to come home. That gray girl? She is excited to come back to you, to complete you. There is work she is ready to help you do, that *you* are ready to do."

I nodded some more and let Amanda help me recline onto the futon once again.

"I want you to journey now," she instructed, "and meet this part of your soul that you have long been estranged from. It's time to welcome her home."

I slipped the mask over my eyes and Amanda began to drum. I dropped into the ethereal shaman world, where my bear greeted me like an old friend. Through the forest I followed him to the stone cottage and I could already tell that everything about it was different. I carried heaps of wildflowers in my arms because Amanda had told me to take an offering to this piece of my soul, and I placed them on the floor of the cottage when I entered. The room was sun filled now, and warm.

The gray girl was standing in the center of the room this time, and she was sparkly and filled with light. For a moment I hesitated before embracing her. I looked back at the door one last time, hoping to see my mother there, but knowing that she was gone. And then I stepped forward and into myself.

Months after all this, standing before the group of motherless daughters, as I conclude my lecture, I am aware that very few of them will undertake the same kinds of journeys I have, with shamanism or psychic mediums or past-life regressions. But I know that's not what is important.

What is important is recognizing that we can lose a piece of ourselves when someone we love dies. And recognizing it is the key to getting it back. The myth of Persephone is just that—a myth. It is a cautionary tale about the ways we can get stuck holding on to someone who has been taken away.

We must learn to live in this world, because we have no other choice. What we do have a choice in is *how* we choose to live. We can remain gray and immobile in the wake of our losses or we can open ourselves up to the world, let the sunshine in, fill our surroundings with heaps of flowers, and know that we loved someone truly and deeply.

## Claire Bidwell Smith

Dear Vera and Jules,

I spent a great many years after my mother died trying to become her in a way. She was a mysterious woman to me, even though we had spent eighteen years together. She was forty when I was born and had seemingly lived a whole lifetime before I came along.

I desperately wanted to know about those years before I was born, about the places she'd lived and the people she'd loved. I wanted to know what she had been like as a teenager, and a young adult. I wanted to know about her first two marriages, her relationships with her parents and her sisters.

I tried to be like her for a long time, even though I wasn't quite sure who that was. I moved to New York City when I was twenty, because that's where she had lived for so many years before I was born.

I visited the apartment building where she had lived, and I looked up old friends of hers. I wrote stories about her and I pored over old photographs that my aunt had unearthed from the back of the closet. I learned how to cook, because my mother had cooked, and I threw parties because that is what she had done.

Finally I realized one day that I am not my mother. I think I had become angry trying so hard to be like her, and frustrated when I couldn't.

The mother-daughter relationship is a complex one. When it is a close one like we share, you will rail against it and simultaneously seek to emulate it. You will despise me, you will think you are supposed to be like me, you will want to be anything but me.

I want you to remember that I am just a woman, like any other. A person, like any other. I am deeply flawed and resiliently human. Even though I have been standing before you all these years, holding open the door to the world, even though I am ushering you into *my* version of the world, it doesn't necessarily have to be the world you inhabit.

I read once that daughters don't become women until they lose their mothers. In some ways I think this is true. This was the case for me. My mother had been so glamorous and charismatic, she'd had such a ferocious presence, that it often drowned out who I was becoming. I knew the world only as she presented it to me, her thoughts and opinions and feelings shaping my own.

When she was gone I was starkly reminded in her absence that I was different from her. I was practical in ways that she was not. I liked things she didn't and disliked others that she did. I kept the kitchen neat while I cooked; my mother destroyed every surface as she worked. I liked to figure out how things worked, whereas my mother often threw up her hands in defeat attempting to use the VCR or hang a painting on the wall.

One afternoon when I was in high school we went to the mall together. My mother was fanatical about securing good parking spaces, and after circling the parking lot for what felt like forever she finally spied a choice space just near the entrance. Just as she was about to pull into it a woman in another car zipped into it, driving the wrong way in the one-way lane to get there.

My mother fumed, and then yelled out her window at the woman, who returned her harsh words with an obscene hand gesture. Furious, my mother drove to the nearest spot in the back of the parking lot and marched us into a candy shop in the mall. She filled a bag with gumballs and then marched us back outside into the hot Florida afternoon, handing me several gumballs.

"Chew," she instructed, filling her own mouth with gum.

We stood next to this woman's car chewing our gum until it had softened, and then my mother instructed me to smear it on her windshield. She did the same with hers, and in that moment I felt giddy, yet also fearful. I remember feeling very much at the whim of this strong woman who was my mother.

She was ferocious like that, wild and impetuous. She was deeply sensitive, but often let her emotions get the best of her. As an adolescent I followed her lead. She was also so very magical and exciting that even frightening moments like this were also exhilarating.

But as I grew older I knew that I was not the same. And today, younger yet than my mother was that day in the parking lot, I know that I could never do such a thing. And to this day, I make a point of always feeling grateful to find a parking spot, no matter how far back in the lot it is.

All of this is just to say that you are not me. Take what works from what I show you about the world, but do not take it as who you are supposed to be. I do have many traits of my mother's. I am my own fierce and brave

## After This

woman, and I am glad to show you that side of myself, but I want you to become your own kinds of brave, your own kinds of wild.

With ferocious love,

*Mama*

# Chapter Eight

There is a small community in central Florida that is composed almost entirely of psychic mediums. It's now overrun with tourists and blinking neon signs offering tarot readings, healing, and communication with the deceased, but Cassadaga was originally founded in 1894, following the popular spiritualism movement of the nineteenth century.

Spiritualism was born in Europe in the 1800s, and based around the belief that the dead are able to communicate with the living. Because spiritualism wasn't exactly a religion and did not come with a set of imposed doctrines, those interested in it did not need to compromise their belief systems in order to incorporate the practice. Thus, it became increasingly popular, even in the United States, during the mid-1800s, when the average life span was around fifty years and it was not uncommon to lose friends and family members at a young age.

There was a swift rise in the movement following the Civil War, when so many people were grieving and desperate to connect with those they had lost. Very quickly, séances, mediums, and the use of Ouija boards became so commonplace that even First Lady Mary Todd Lincoln held séances in the White House following the death of her eleven-year-old son, William. Spiritualism offered an immediate kind of comfort, and gave the hope of continued communication with lost loved ones.

Spiritualism holds the belief that the soul continues to exist after it leaves the physical body, and that after death, the soul continues to grow and evolve. Table-turning parties, in which participants would gather around a table together and place their hands on it, attempting to communicate with the deceased and receiving messages from movement that caused the table to shake or objects to overturn, were some of the initial forms of communication. And in 1886 the Associated Press ran an article about an Ohio-based spiritualist camp where attendees were using a board containing letters of the alphabet to communicate with the dead.

Entrepreneur Charles Kennard read the article and jumped on it, and in 1891 the Kennard Novelty Company put a product on the market that would change everything: the Ouija board. It was priced at $1.50 and was described as a magical device that would answer questions about "the past, present and future with marvelous accuracy," providing a connection "between the known and unknown, the material and immaterial."

Ouija boards have been on the market ever since, and have not really changed much, today's modern boards still comprising the same format of letters and numbers that the original contained. In fact, Ouija boards are for sale in Cassadaga, alongside crystal balls, dream catchers, and "ghost-hunting" equipment.

I peruse through all manner of these goods as I wait for my first appointment with a medium down the street. I'm staying at the Cassadaga Hotel, right in the heart of the little community, and it's an old, spooky kind of place. It's mid-March and surprisingly cool for Florida. Spanish moss hangs from the trees that line the streets and dragonflies buzz through the air.

## After This

In a book about the history of Cassadaga I read that in 1894, following a message he'd received in a séance, a man named George Colby traveled through the wilderness of Central Florida, led by a spirit guide, until he came across the land upon which he founded the Cassadaga Spiritualist Camp. According to the Cassadaga website, the camp consists of "approximately 57 acres with 55 residences." And although "residents may own their homes . . . the church retains ownership of the land. . . . About 25 of the Camp's residents are mediums who offer counseling from their homes."

I first heard about Cassadaga after watching an HBO documentary called *No One Dies in Lily Dale*, about a similar community in upstate New York. The idea was utterly fascinating to me: an entire town devoted to mediumship and communication with the dead. I had to see it for myself.

On the way to a book conference in Martin County, Florida, I detour so that I can spend a night in Cassadaga, and decide to show up with nothing more than a hotel reservation. I'm accompanied by my skeptic friend, Wendy. She's fascinated by my obsession with this stuff, but reluctant to believe any of it herself. We check in to our sparsely furnished room and then head over to the camp bookstore across the street.

It's your typical new age bookshop, full of crystals and incense, shelves upon shelves of books about angels and psychics and afterlife communication. I've been drawn to these bookstores since I was a teenager, and over the years I've found that they're all the same. There's always a cat, and always a display of crystal balls. There are little bins of colorful stones by the cash register, alongside angel bookmarks and kitschy items like tiny cases of EnlightenMints to freshen your breath before a reading.

In the back of the Cassadaga bookstore there is a room with chairs and an old telephone still plugged into the wall. Above the telephone is an elaborate display of business cards featuring all the various mediums in town who are available to meet that day. A sign below the cards advises that you should read through them all, and then follow your gut instinct on which medium to contact. I spend a long time looking at the various cards, trying to feel some kind of connection with the various names offered.

Over and over I'm drawn to a medium named Claire Van Cott, but I feel like that's silly, and must be only because we have the same name. I take her card though, along with a few others, and then place calls to all of them to make appointments. The only one I can't get through to is Claire, but I leave her a message, feeling even more of a sense of urgency that she is the one I should see.

My first appointment is with a man named Richard Russell, and I leave Wendy to have lunch at the hotel while I walk down the street to his house. All of the houses are an old, Victorian style, and the overcast day lends a creepy vibe to the neighborhood. Random people walk by alone or in groups and I am conscious that even though they appear like tourists, many of them are likely grieving and are here because they deeply miss someone they love.

Richard Russell's house is a two-story Victorian, like the rest on the street, and I take a seat on the screened-in porch while I wait for him. There are old dolls placed about, and a large Raggedy Ann sits on a mildew-covered porch swing that creaks in the faint breeze. Russell finally opens the front door and ushers me into the house, and it's like stepping back in time. The rooms are filled with musty antique furniture, and papers lie piled about in various rooms. I follow him back to his office and take a seat on a dilapidated couch.

Richard is in his late fifties, heavyset, and labored in his physical movements. I have seen so many mediums at this point that I have no real expectations, nor a strong desire to necessarily receive a message. I am here mostly from a place of curiosity. After Richard gets comfortable he asks if I've done this before. I nod and wait for more. Even though my expectations are low, there is still a lingering hope that something amazing will happen.

However, he spends the next hour of our time together simply lecturing to me about spiritualism and how our modern age of technology has led us far away from our natural ability to communicate with other planes of existence. He drones on about his experiences with the spirit realm, offering me no insight to my personal life or losses, and concludes by urging me to follow a path of meditation. He also tells me that I can call him anytime for more sessions by telephone.

I leave and try not to think about the sixty dollars I just handed him, and I head back to the hotel to meet Wendy. I can't decide if the mediums that have nothing concrete to offer, like Richard Russell, are just burned out, or if they're utter quacks to begin with. I shrug off the session and downplay my disappointment to Wendy, wanting her to remain open to possibly having a good experience if she chooses to see a psychic herself while we're here.

We walk across the street the other way to another psychic bookshop and I make an appointment with a tarot reader. Wendy and I glance over all the books and the ghost-hunting equipment displayed on a shelf, which includes electronic voice phenomenon (EVP) recorders and full-spectrum cameras. I'm still feeling this pull to speak with Claire Van Cott, so while I wait for my tarot reading I give her another call, but again I get her answering service. I decide to just walk down to her house and see if she is there. All of the mediums' addresses are right there on their cards and I see that her house is next to the camp bookstore.

As I approach, I see a woman sitting on the screened-in porch, and as I get closer she looks up at me. "Claire?" she asks across the distance.

"Yes," I say. "Are you Claire?"

"Yes," she replies, and we both laugh. "I was just about to call you," she says, standing up to talk to me. It turns out that she is fully booked for the rest of the day, but she tells me that she feels compelled to find time to speak with me. Normally this kind of thing makes me squirm, feeling certain that this is something all mediums say, but in this case, I feel the same compulsion. We make an appointment for the next morning.

That afternoon I have a session with the tarot card reader, who, like Richard Russell, tells me nothing interesting. She talks vaguely about my marriage and life path, but the things she tells me seem like things she could be saying to anyone. That night at the hotel Wendy and I discuss the afterlife. She is actually my literary agent, but over the years that we've worked together we have formed a deep friendship, Wendy offering a motherly presence in my life that I am grateful for.

Wendy was drawn to my book when I submitted it to her because she had seen her teenage daughters through the grief following their father's death years ago, and as a result, my story had resonated with her. As we talk about her daughters' experiences and grief processes I think about what a particular world loss can thrust you into. Over the course of my first book's release I've heard equally from people wondering how I could be so affected by these losses and others who have written to me with gratitude for allowing them to feel okay about their own lengthy bereavement processes.

I'm still thinking about all this the next morning when I walk over to Claire Van Cott's little house. It's more like a small studio apartment in a two-story building, and Claire explains that she doesn't live in town, that she just uses this space for her readings. She's in her midforties, on the heavier side, and has warm eyes that crinkle at the edges when she smiles at me. She bustles about the

## After This

tiny room and I take out my phone to record the session, asking her permission first.

Claire begins with a simple meditation, asking me to envision a soft purple light flowing through my chakra system. I'm still a little muddy on chakras in general, but I've gone to enough meditation and yoga classes to picture my seven chakra energy spheres, and I try to imagine a light flowing through my torso, activating them all. For a moment I muse on how easily I do these things now, even when I'm not sure what, exactly, I'm doing.

Claire has asked me if I would like a psychic life reading session or a medium reading, or a little of both. I tell her I would like a little of both, knowing that whenever you get a medium reading it always turns into a little of both anyway, your deceased loved ones coming through with messages about your life, your state of health, and future projects.

She closes her eyes and takes some deep breaths. I think back to my session with Delphina in Chicago and how nervous I was, how monumental it seemed to be visiting a medium in the first place, compared to how I feel now with so many of these sessions under my belt.

"I feel an older woman coming through, perhaps a grandmother," Claire tells me.

I smile, remembering how my grandmother came through in that first reading with John Edward as well. It seems fitting that she would. When she was alive, particularly after my mother died, she always made a point of making sure I knew she was thinking about me.

"Your grandmother is telling me that you've been keeping yourself busy to the point of exhaustion," Claire says with her eyes still closed. "But that you're on a mission, very purposeful, something very purposeful. She's talking about you running yourself ragged to the point of exhaustion, though. Are you writing a good deal? Are you working on a book of some sort?"

"I am. All of that," I say. "I'm working on a book right now and I'm running myself ragged."

"Your grandma wants you to take care of yourself," Claire murmurs.

I smile again, and take a deep breath. I know she's right. My life has felt nonstop lately with travel, and taking care of my daughters, and trying to get this book done. It's been weeks since I've made it to a yoga class or gotten a full night's sleep. It's nice to imagine my grandmother seeing all of this and worrying about me.

"There's an older gentleman here as well now," Claire says, breaking my reverie. "He's around the same age as your grandmother, so I'm thinking maybe it's her spouse, although that doesn't feel quite right."

"It could be my father," I tell her. "He was actually close in age to my grandmother."

"That does seem to make more sense," she says, closing her eyes again and seeming to tune in to whatever frequency she's listening to.

"Would your dad have called you his little girl?" she asks, and I nod. "There's a bit of a sad note of your dad's passing," she continues. "Your dad feels that you have never quite gotten over the whole thing."

"Um, I don't know. His death was very peaceful for me in a lot of ways," I reply.

"Yes, I'm getting that," Claire says. "But there's a certain bit of you and your ambition that is charged with your relationship with your father. Your work is driven by the fact that you want to show you are your father's girl."

I nod again. It's true, I think to myself. Although I was able to face his death in a much braver way than I had with my mother, his loss still lives with me, and I am always conscious of him when it

## After This

comes to the work I put into the world, wanting to make him proud and carry on his legacy.

Claire becomes emotional here, actual tears running down her face. "Oh, you had a beautiful relationship with him, didn't you?" she murmurs. "He's showing me that you really enjoyed each other's company. It was a very nice, sweet relationship."

I begin to cry as well. I did have a sweet relationship with my father, and so often I've found myself grateful that I lost my mother first so that I could have those years in which to get to know him. We truly did just enjoy spending time with each other. Tears are rolling down my face now too, and I feel a deep sense of longing for my father's presence in my current life, something I don't often allow myself to feel.

"He wants you to pace yourself a little more. He's saying you don't have a back-off point, and that you're going to hit an emotional wall," Claire says.

When she says this I flash to a recent session I had with a client in my practice. This client is a young woman in her twenties who lost her mother when she was in college. Her father was never a presence in her life and now she is very much on her own, living in Los Angeles, and consumed by her work with nonprofits.

This client arrived in my office the previous week, feeling utterly overwhelmed by her life, also not really having a back-off point. From my perspective, it was easy to recognize the problem, but I knew that she could not see it herself. After she had explained to me all of her work frustrations and how she was struggling to find any time for herself, I let her take a breath and then I asked just one simple question.

"What would it be like if your mother was still in your life right now?" I proposed.

Immediately her eyes filled with tears and for several minutes she sat silently, taking breaths and letting the tears run down her cheeks. I let silence hang over the room until she was ready to speak again.

"Yes," she said finally. "That's exactly it. I don't have that presence of unconditional love in my life," she explained. "All the love and support in my life right now comes on a conditional basis through my devotion to all this work." She continued to cry for a while longer, and I knew that this was an important moment of recognition for her.

It was easy to see it from my vantage point, because it's something I struggle with myself. When my mother died, my reaction was to not *need* a mother anymore, when in fact what I most needed was to learn to mother myself. This push to stake my independence had only grown stronger after my father died, and it was years before I was able to recognize that I needed to learn to nurture myself in their absence.

"You need balances and checks, your father is saying," Claire tells me, and I tune back in to the session, pushing the thoughts of my client away. "Your list is a mile long."

I nod and for the first time in a while I let myself really feel how much I miss him, and how different my life would be if he were still here. I think about the security I would feel if he were here, the presence, much like my client is missing, of security and unconditional love that he would provide.

Claire is crying again, her voice fraught with emotion. "Yes, the love with you guys is so strong. He's so giving to you. Start to acknowledge his presence more often. You need a sense that your dad is still here. He's over there, yes," she says, referring to the spirit world, "but he's still very, very close to you."

In that moment, in that room in Cassadaga with Claire Van

## After This

Cott, I let myself feel my father's presence, his closeness, the love he always had for me, all of it still swimming around me.

"I would suggest that you talk to him much more often," Claire says. "Acknowledge that closeness. Acknowledge his presence."

Months from now when I listen to this recording I'll cry again, and when I'm done with the transcription I'll light a candle at my little altar table and I'll close my eyes and again let myself feel my father swimming around me.

At the end of my session with Claire Van Cott I pay her sixty dollars and head out into the sunny Florida morning, feeling that there is something very worthwhile in these sessions when they're good, like this one has been. We must allow ourselves to feel the presence of our lost loved ones, I think as I walk back across the street to the hotel, where Wendy is waiting to meet me. Even if it is simulated or imagined, the relationships themselves were real and they are still a part of our lives. Being reminded of that, by whatever means, is vital.

I watch a couple of tourists walk into the bookshop, thinking about this place, Cassadaga. It's utterly kooky and strange, but it's important too. This is life. This is death. This is love.

A few months later I decide to hold a séance in my house. I'm feeling inspired by my visit to Cassadaga, and by my readings about the nineteenth-century spiritualism movement. At one point in history it was practically commonplace to hold séances, so why not try it myself?

Attempting to contact the dead on my own accord seems like the final piece of this puzzle. A couple of years ago I briefly attended a weekly "spirit circle" at a dusty new age shop in Santa Monica, where I gathered every Sunday afternoon with a random assortment of participants, all women, in the back of the store. I had found the group after a little Internet research, and it had been billed as a way to enhance and explore "mediumship abilities" in a relaxed setting.

At the first session I took a seat on a wobbly folding chair and introduced myself as a writer who was working on a book about the afterlife. The rest of the attendants were a motley assortment of women who ranged in age from twenty to sixty-five. They were spiritualists and healers, therapists and gardeners. All of them claimed to have psychic abilities and connections with the spirit realm that they wished to further develop.

Each week we would begin with a long meditation, opening our chakra systems to different lights and energies, and then calling on our lost loved ones to come forth. After that we would sit in silence, various participants voicing different impressions or images that came to them. Most of them were vague and did not elicit responses from anyone in the group, but every once in a while one of the women would come forth with a few uncanny details that resonated with someone's deceased loved one.

Nothing particularly interesting ever happened for me in the group, although I tried really hard to open myself up to the idea that it could. I was pregnant with Juliette at the time, and I would sit in silence with the group, trying not to focus on the baby kicking around in my belly, instead trying to relax my mind, letting images and feelings come through. But nothing I voiced aloud to the group ever resonated with anyone, and I finally quit going close to the time my daughter was born.

I had enjoyed the group, though, fascinated by the idea that it might be possible for anyone to cultivate psychic abilities. It does indeed seem like something that would take practice, and I wondered,

## After This

if I were to work at it long enough, whether I might be able to tap into a more intuitive side of myself. I muse on this thought again as I make plans to host my séance, the idea of doing so having occurred to me more than once.

Every time I thought about holding a séance, though, I felt a little nervous. In all of my research so far, I have come across many tidbits about negative or dark energies that could come through when attempting to connect with the spirit realm. And even though I'm reluctant to buy into the horror movie idea of ghosts and demons, I still feel cautious. Just because I don't believe in them doesn't mean they're not real. Every time I pictured holding a séance in my house I stalled, worrying about bringing some kind of unwanted entity into my life.

But still, the idea remained in the back of my mind, so when I receive word that my friend Cat Kabira, from Bali, is coming to town, I ask her if she's up for helping me conduct a séance in my house. Cat has been studying shamanism for almost two decades, working with various indigenous shamans in South America and participating in countless ceremonies all over the world. She is rich in knowledge and skill about creating safe spaces in which to do spiritual work, and I feel confident that with her presence, anything I attempt on my own will be protected.

As soon as I get Cat's nod of approval and promise of attendance, I feel a buzz of excitement and I go about making my plans. First I order a Ouija board, and a book called *How to Communicate with Spirits: Séances, Ouija Boards and Summoning*, by Angela Kaelin. I choose a night when my daughters will not be in the house, and then I begin making a list of people to invite.

Several friends immediately come to mind and I text them a simple message: "I'm having a séance! Want to come?"

Their responses mirror my own feelings of excitement, and my phone lights up within minutes.

"Duh. Of course," one of my best friends, Jillian, texts.

"Absolutely," my friend Mick replies.

"I think I've been waiting my whole life to get this text," Jenny responds. "Yes, yes, yes."

My friend Christa texts back, "Whoa! Yes!" And then she adds, "Did I tell you I was once a telephone psychic?"

Just based on their responses, I feel confident that I've invited the right people. If anything, my only requirement is that attendees are open and enthusiastic about the experience.

As the date nears I grow more and more excited, wondering why I haven't done this sooner. I page through my book, reading about the old spiritualism séances done in the 1800s, and how best to use the Ouija board as a means of communication. There are all kinds of suggestions in the book for how to approach séances. It advises against the use of alcohol or drugs, suggests drinking plenty of water, and even offers some recipes for electrolyte-enhancing beverages that may come in handy.

The book also advises that participants should make a point to invite their lost loved ones to the séance before the actual event, allowing energy to build up in advance. I like this idea, and a few days before the séance I e-mail my friends.

> Hi Ladies,
>
> I'm so excited and grateful that you'll be joining me for the séance on Tuesday.
>
> There will be 8 of us, all women, and I think it's going to be an amazing group. I know each of you will bring something really special to the experience. Thank you again for agreeing to participate.

## After This

The point of the séance is kind of a culmination of all the work I've been doing the last few years to attempt to understand and connect with the afterlife. I could have found a medium to hire to join us, but the goal is to try to do this on a kind of amateur level. Can *we laywomen* connect with the afterlife? is the real question. My dear friend Cat Kabira will be here from Bali, and without her I wouldn't feel comfortable attempting this on our own, or in my house, for that matter, but I know that Cat will be able to help us keep a safe space for whatever we delve into.

I want to do a kind of old-school spiritualism table reading. I've got a Ouija board and a bunch of candles. In preparation, I'd love for all of you to spend some time in the next couple of days thinking about who you might want to contact and asking them in advance to join us at the séance and come through. Please feel free to bring photographs or objects belonging to that person, and also any other objects you might think will be useful to the séance.

Let's plan to convene at my house at 7:30 on Tuesday evening.

I'd also like to ask that you don't drink or take any mind-altering substances prior to the séance. Everything I've read seems to suggest that a clear, sober head is best for this stuff. We'll drink plenty of wine afterward, I'm sure.

Hit me up with any questions or concerns. Otherwise, I'm looking forward to this!

xoxo,

*Claire*

On the morning of the séance I go about cleaning my house, clearing off my dining room table, and digging out an enormous pack of tea lights from Ikea. I'm filled with anticipation and curiosity about what is going to happen. Strangely I feel an utter lack of apprehension. And although there is an undeniably fun element to all of this, I'm also taking it very seriously.

I spend the morning of the séance gathering items that belonged to the various people I would like to connect with—my mother, Julie, my father, and my friend Abby, who died of breast cancer just a month ago at age thirty-seven. I take out a necklace that Abby gave me, find an old shirt of Julie's, one of my mother's rings, and my father's wallet. I run my fingers over each of these things, feeling full of love for the people I miss, and I place each object next to a photo of that person.

It's nice to do this, to simply take out these items and look at them, touch them, remember the person to whom they belonged. It seems odd to me that these things can exist still, without the person they once belonged to. I stand at a little table in my dining room and light some candles. Then I take a moment to hold each object belonging to my loved ones, focusing on them, and silently inviting their owners to join us that evening. Tears run down my face as I picture each of them.

I see my mother pursing her lips in the car mirror after she applies a layer of lipstick. I hear Julie's soft voice on the telephone, the way she used to answer when I called. I picture my father in his office chair, swiveling around to greet me as I arrive at his condo. And I envision the way Abby used to walk up the sidewalk to my house, a bright smile on her face as she strode toward me. I miss them all deeply. My heart feels full with the thought that even if I can't quite see them in real life, maybe they can feel me thinking about them wherever they are.

## After This

That evening my friends show up promptly at seven thirty. Cat is staying with me and together we greet each guest on my patio with a hug. Jillian Lauren arrives first. I met her ten years ago through Dave Eggers's literacy organization, 826LA. She's the author of a memoir called *Some Girls* and a novel called *Pretty*, and is finishing up her third book, about adopting her son from Ethiopia. My close bond with Jillian comes from a place of sharing the challenge of navigating motherhood and writing. We meet often to talk about our lives and I know she shares a similar curiosity about the deeper picture of life.

Christa Parravani arrives next, author of the memoir *Her*, about her twin sister's death. Christa is a new friend, but we made a quick connection, and after reading her book about her own search to reconcile her grief upon losing her sister, I knew she would be a good fit for this group.

After Christa, my friend Mick shows up. She and I get together often to talk about our work. A therapist and a mother, Mick is a seeker, and has a deeply spiritual side. She has delved into all sorts of past-life regressions and shamanism.

Jenny Feldon arrives after Mick. She is also a mother to two young children, and the author of a memoir called *Karma Gone Bad*, about her time in India when her husband was relocated for work. Like the rest of these women, Jenny feels like a sister to me, and people often remark on how much we look alike. I marvel at the fact that four of us in attendance have written memoirs, knowing it is a sign of introspection that I am drawn to.

My friend Joan Lynch arrives, hilariously sardonic yet always thoughtful. Joan has worked in broadcast journalism for many years and has seen her fair share of personal and national tragedy. She has a serious spiritual side, and we've had many long talks about God, and about powers greater than we can perhaps perceive. I smile when I see her, knowing that she will bring a thoughtful energy to the group.

Lisa Whelan arrives last. I met her through a group of parents I'm friends with, and she has always shown a particular interest in my afterlife quest, having spent a lot of time thinking about it on her own. She's excited to be part of this group, and has in fact come straight from the funeral of her uncle. She shows up with an enormous bouquet of funeral flowers to contribute, and we all laugh.

We spend the next half hour sitting around on the patio, discussing the plan. As this is our first time gathering together as a group, all of them having simply agreed to be here after my initial text, I want to hear a bit about their expectations, ideas, and any fears or concerns. No one in the group voices any hesitation, and so we go over my notes and ideas for how to proceed. Christa shares a story about a séance she attended in her twenties, in which she and her friends used a Ouija board to contact a friend who had committed suicide. This friend came through with concrete messages and information that proved true following the séance, and we all marvel at her story.

I read aloud a couple of points I found interesting in my book about séances. The first one emphasizes that it takes time for the psychic energy in the room to build up, and cautions that we should not expect anything elaborate to happen for at least forty-five minutes. The second point is a reminder that the connections we make with the other side can come in various forms, including hearing things in the room, seeing objects move, or even, for some, feeling various impressions or thoughts in our bodies. I encourage my friends to voice anything unusual that they think or feel during our session.

Finally I stand, indicating that it's time to go inside. I take a moment, looking around at these women, and thank them for coming so readily to this experience. I think about my mother in that moment, and feel gratitude for the way she modeled female friendships for me. Over the course of my adult life the women in it have truly supported me in every way possible, and this group is no exception.

Inside we convene excitedly around the dining room table, where I have lit a dozen tea lights and placed the Ouija board. All the other lights in the house are off, and it has grown dark outside. There is a giddy sense in the air and we all look around at each other, candlelight casting a warm glow on our faces.

Cat starts us off with an opening meditation and prayer. She asks that we make a little offering to the spirits, like they do in Bali, placing flowers, a few bits of candy, and some loose tobacco on a plate next to the glowing candles.

In a soft voice, Cat reminds us, "Part of the ability to call in and to hear, and to feel, is to remember that we are more than these three-dimensional creatures. We are interdimensional, and there are parts of all of us that are constantly connecting with the spirit world. Take this moment," she says, "a moment that allows you to be open to all the parts of yourself that feel and see and know.

"We ask permission tonight," she continues, "that in a safe way and in a loving way we connect to our loved ones. We ask that only those with the highest vibration, only those with the same vibration of love can come through. We call in for protection and guidance from Buddha and Jesus and we give you offerings of flowers. We know that this is something that is serious, that is not to be taken lightly. We ask to be guided, that we only stay in the spaces that are in the same vibration of love. And for all the beings that want to come through, for every woman in this room, we ask for your permission."

I smile, with my eyes closed, grateful for Cat's calm and loving presence. After a moment of silence we all open our eyes and look around the table. The candles flicker across the faces smiling back at me.

"Should I do the invocation now?" I ask, and Cat nods at me. I catch Jenny's eye across the table and she has a mischievous look on her face. On the patio we talked about the 1996 movie *The Craft*, which depicts four teenage girls who formed a coven in high school, and I know that Jenny is thinking about a particular scene in which one of the girls in the film recites a similar invocation to the one I am about to read from *How to Communicate with Spirits*.

> *We call upon the Four Elements and the Watchtowers to oversee this operation.*
> 
> *We open this circle as a consecrated place of love and knowledge.*
> 
> *Guardians of the Watchtowers of the East, share your wisdom with us.*
> 
> *Guardians of the Watchtowers of the South, bring us love, harmony, and goodness.*
> 
> *Guardians of the Watchtowers of the West, give us your protection.*
> 
> *Guardians of the Watchtowers of the North, fulfill our needs.*
> 
> *By the power of Air, Fire, Water, and Earth, bless this circle and all who stand within it.*
> 
> *By the power of three times three, so mote it be!*

Finally it's time to begin. I feel that I should be the one to open communication first, but I feel nervous, and a sense of performance anxiety sweeps through me. I have invited all these women here, made a big deal about this whole thing. What if we can't really connect with the dead?

I take a breath, trying to release my expectations, and I tell the

## After This

group that I'd like to begin by trying to contact my friend Abby, who has recently died. I pass around her photo and talk a bit about my friendship with her. The women at the table take turns looking at the photo and listening to my recounting of our relationship.

As a group we already decided that it would be best for two people who are not the questioner to take over the Ouija board, so I pass it to Mick and Jillian.

"Abby," I say aloud in the hushed room, "I'd like to invite you to come through and connect with us."

Mick and Jillian are sitting perfectly still with their fingers on the unmoving planchette.

"I don't know if I really have a question," I say aloud to Abby, "other than wondering if you're okay, and if you have any messages for me or your family."

Abby's death was a hard one. She died of breast cancer eleven months after being diagnosed. She was only thirty-seven years old, and left behind her husband and two small children. I spent a lot of time with her in those last weeks, and she was so fearful about leaving her family behind. Every time I came home from visiting her I wept, overcome with sadness and fear for her. It's been six weeks since her death and I miss her deeply.

The planchette underneath Jillian and Mick's fingertips begins to move and we all lean forward in our seats to watch. It sways from letter to letter, selecting a random assortment. I write them down in my notebook and there is a hush over the room as we wait for something concrete.

"Maybe ask something more specific," Cat suggests.

"Abby, are you okay?" I ask aloud.

Nothing.

"Are we sure that this is Abby?" Cat asks.

"Abby, is this you?" I ask.

For another ten minutes the Ouija board just continues to select random letters. Finally we decide to pass it to the other end of the table, to let someone else try to connect. Jillian calls upon her friend Jennifer, who died several years ago of an overdose. She passes around a photo of her and talks about what a bright, energetic woman she was. She laughs as she tells us that her friend would have fit right in at this table of women.

Cat and Lisa have their hands on the board and Jillian softly invites her friend to join us. She asks her how she is and if she has any messages for us. Again, the board picks out an innocuous assortment of letters.

We've been at this for half an hour so far, and nothing concrete has happened. The room is hushed as we all watch the board with anticipation, and my stomach rumbles, reminding me that I forgot to eat dinner. We give up on Jillian's friend and decide to move on to someone else.

We pass the board to Jillian and Christa, and we begin asking aloud if there are any spirits that would like to come through. The planchette is moving swiftly underneath their hands now and we all lean forward, watching. Over and over it points out the letters C and Z. We ask if there is a spirit here to speak with us and it moves to "yes." We ask whom it is here for and it shifts around to another random spelling that means nothing to any of us.

"Is it you, Aunt Alice?" Mick asks.

It moves to "no."

"Is it you, uncle?" Lisa asks.

"Why don't you tell us about your uncle?" I say to her.

She tells us about his life and about the memorial she attended that day.

We ask the board if he is with us. This time it answers yes, but when we ask for a message we again get gibberish. The board goes to the letter G over and over again.

"Maybe it's my dad," I say. "His name was Gerry."

"That's kind of what I keep getting," Cat says. "That it's your dad."

"Dad," I say, "are you here?" It feels strange to talk to him out loud like this.

The board gives us nothing. We're an hour into our session now and everyone is getting a little restless.

"I keep getting this sense that the Ouija board is too limited for spirit contact," I say finally.

"I'm feeling the same thing," Cat says. "I can definitely feel the presence of spirits in the room wanting to come through, but I don't know if the Ouija board is the right medium."

"Maybe we should just all close our eyes and see what we can feel," I suggest, thinking back to the spirit circle and to all the mediums I've seen who have not used any tools like Ouija boards.

We all close our eyes and sit in silence. After a while several of the women begin announcing various sensations or images that come to them, but nothing really resonates. I hear Mick's stomach grumble beside me and I laugh a little. She laughs too.

"Did you say you put out cheese and crackers, Claire?" Mick asks.

"Yes," I say, laughing. "I'm starving too," I admit.

We decide that it's time to pour some wine and eat a little. The thinking behind not drinking or taking mind-altering substances in the literature I've read suggests that the act of doing so lowers one's vibration, potentially allowing negative energy into the circle, but we unanimously decide that perhaps it will serve to loosen us up a bit, all of us having spent the past hour feeling quite stiff and serious.

Soon we are sitting around the table, candles still aglow, drinking wine and passing a platter of cheese and crackers back and forth.

We abandon the Ouija board for a time, relaxing into stories about the people we lost and telling anecdotes about our time with them. The energy in the room has decidedly shifted, and we are jovial and full of laughter.

After a while the group begins to break up, women getting up to use the bathroom, Mick going out onto the patio to make a phone call, but those of us still seated decide to pick up the Ouija board again.

At the end of the table, just before we devolved into dinner party mode, both Cat and Jenny Feldon reported feeling a lot of strange energy, so we pass the board back to them. I'm opening another bottle of wine, working to refill the empty glasses at my end of the table, when I look over and see the planchette moving across the board.

Except neither Jenny's nor Cat's fingers are on it; their hands are poised just above it, preparing to begin.

"Whoa!" Jenny exclaims. "Did you see that?"

We all did, and we watch as they place their fingers on it for real now, asking if there is a spirit that would like to come through. The planchette moves swiftly to "yes," and a hush falls over our group.

"Can you tell us your name?" Cat asks.

Before they can get any further, Mick comes back into the house and tells us that she needs to go home to help with her daughter. The planchette stops moving and the group begins to break up, Joan leaving as well.

Cat, Jenny, Jillian, Lisa, Christa, and I move to the living room, where we sit in a circle around my coffee table, giving one last attempt at the Ouija board. Again, Cat and Jenny sit down with it, Jenny describing how she felt an outside pressure coming through her arms when she was still at the dining room table.

"I shit you not," she says. "It was the weirdest feeling I've ever experienced."

## After This

Cat nods. "I totally felt it too."

We take one more shot at the Ouija board, but again we get nothing concrete. It's close to midnight at this point and we decide to officially call an end to the séance. I hug my friends good-bye and blow out the candles. There are empty wine bottles and drips of candle wax scattered across the house. Although nothing really evocative happened, I have a deep sense of peace and love as I go to bed that night. Not to mention that I sleep like the dead.

In the days following the séance I receive notes and messages from my friends who attended, all of them expressing the same sentiment, one of gratitude for being allowed to share in the created space of honoring our loved ones. I am reminded of that class in grad school when we were asked to talk with one another about what happens when we die, and I recall my friends at the séance simply having the opportunity to share stories about their dead friends and relatives, all of us passing around those photos and objects that had once belonged to them.

That night, at the séance, the act of simply creating a space in which to honor these people and our love for them felt profound. The spooky element, which I think deters so many people from holding such an event, was washed away by all the love and reverence our group held for one another, and for this ritual.

I don't think I want to start holding séances regularly, but I do think that nights like this one are something I want to bring into my life more often. The morning after the séance I carefully put away all the objects belonging to my mother and father, and to Julie and Abby, feeling grateful that I had a chance to revisit them.

I pause at the door of my closet, wondering if they can see me in that moment, in my little house in Santa Monica. I imagine how good it must feel to them to know how much they are still loved and missed in this realm, and for a moment I let myself feel them loving me back.

By all reports, Elisabeth Kübler-Ross got a little spooky in her later years. She became seemingly obsessed with the afterlife, conducting her own séances, researching near-death survivors, and even attempting to have some of her own consciousness-out-of-body experiences.

Is this what I'm doing? Am I totally losing it? I wonder often as I continue to delve into this realm. Am I going too far over the edge into this obsession with death and what happens next? All the psychic mediums and meditation and past-life regressions and attempts to communicate with the dead . . . all of it sometimes makes me feel like I'm going crazy.

I look at the people around me, living their lives in normal, dutiful ways. Going to work, raising their children, falling in and out of love, making trips to the grocery store and to weddings out of state, celebrating birthdays, and I wonder why I can't be like that. Why can't I just settle into this life, *my* life, and be a regular mom and person?

And the answer I always come to is one that Kübler-Ross faced as well. When you've gone through something traumatic, when you've faced death and loss as much as we have, it's only natural that it changes your entire view of life. How can you lose someone as vital as a parent or a spouse or a child and then just go back to your regular life?

You can't. You must attempt to make sense of it. You must make meaning of it. You must peel back all the layers of your life that once so carefully kept you going to the grocery store and weddings and preschool drop-off. For these are the very things that suddenly seem so strange in the face of death and loss. But they are also the very things we must return to, because this is what life is, this moving through the years and loves and obligations and various paths we all take.

Elisabeth Kübler-Ross, an identical triplet, was born in 1926 in Zurich. She credited being a triplet for shaping much of who she was. She claimed to have felt utterly replaceable, which she believed set her on a search for meaning and purpose in life. A defiant and strong-willed young woman, she left home at age sixteen and embarked on a series of experiences that would continue to aid her on her path to becoming the foremost expert on grief and loss in our modern culture.

Following WWII, Kübler-Ross served as a volunteer in war-torn countries, assisting in hospitals and refugee centers. A visit to the Majdanek concentration camp in Poland, where she saw hundreds of images of butterflies carved into the walls by children who once resided there, was one that stayed with her throughout her lifetime, informing her work and her thoughts about death. She would go on to use the caterpillar-cocoon-butterfly metaphor in many of her lectures and writings about death and the afterlife, writing that "death is but a transition from this life to another existence."

Her seminal work, *On Death and Dying*, was published in 1969, and the five-stage process she outlined within is what she remains known for today. Over the course of her lifetime and work, Dr. Kübler-Ross faced much criticism and even ridicule. Yet she forged ahead, intent on making death more acceptable in our culture.

In her later years, she dove into research about near-death experiences, meeting with countless individuals who had gone to the brink and come back with stories of light and love and a feeling of knowing that the soul continues. Kübler-Ross had her own near-death experiences, induced iatrogenically, in a laboratory in Virginia. What she felt and saw during those out-of-body experiences gave her a peace and a devout faith that consciousness is not dependent on the physical form, that our human lives are only a small portion of our soul's experience in the world.

Her conclusion after these years of work was that when we die and leave the physical body there is an immediate absence of fear and anxiety, and that we go on to experience a higher awareness of a "cosmic consciousness" that we are all part of. She writes that we never die alone, because once we leave the physical realm there are no limits of time or space. We are immediately with those who have passed before us, and we are able to transcend the constraints that once held us in the physical world, allowing us to visit those who are still living.

Kübler-Ross returns to the butterfly metaphor, insisting that when we die a physical death we briefly enter a spiritual cocoon, from which we emerge into a different plane of existence. We initially enter a period of review, during which we are "held responsible for everything we have done. . . . In this total, unconditional love we will have to review not only every deed of our life, but also . . . how every thought, word and deed and choice of our total life has affected others." She writes, "Our life is literally nothing but a school, where we are tested, where we are put through the tumbler. And it is *our* choice, and no one else's choice, whether we come out of the tumbler crushed or polished."

Kübler-Ross claims that it is during this process that we become aware of our potential, and we learn that everything we experienced during our physical lives was a series of lessons we needed to learn on a soul level. She writes that life "is a school where we choose our own minor and major, where we choose our own teachers, where all of us have to go through tests, trials and tribulations. And when we have passed the tests, we are allowed to graduate and return back home

## After This

where we all came from and where we all will be reunited again one day."

I immediately google iatrogenics after reading about Kübler-Ross's experiences, even though I know that I don't need to have a near-death experience to recognize that my beliefs about life and what happens when we die have already changed. "You do not need to go to India, and you do not need LSD or mescaline or psilocybin in order to change your life," Kübler-Ross writes. "You do not need to do anything except be responsible for your choices."

I take a deep breath when I read this, realizing that at this point I've really just succumbed to this stuff. I think I really believe what she says about life after death, and that I've come to believe what they've all been saying all along—James Van Praagh and Gahl, Rabbi Mendel and Nan the shaman. The beliefs I once held about this life being all there is seem naive and unnecessarily restrictive. I've had enough experiences now to know that I don't know. I don't know what happens when we die, but I now firmly believe that this physical form is not the end.

Kübler-Ross is right. Rabbi Mendel is right. We don't have to know the answers. We don't need to know our exact path. All we have to do is make the right choices right here and now. We have to live a life we feel good about. We have to strive to live in the present moment, to teach our children and loved ones to make the world a better place, through our own examples of doing exactly that.

## Claire Bidwell Smith

Dear Girls,

My mother used to tell me that only stupid people get bored. I think she was right. There is so much in the world to be curious about.

Be curious about yourself. Be curious about others. Be curious about the world. Ask questions, take nothing at face value, don't be afraid to search for what you think might be possible.

Here's a tip. Whenever you're in a situation where you're meeting new people and you don't know what to say, just ask them about themselves. People love to talk about themselves. Ask them where they're from, what they like to do, where they've traveled recently. They'll have a million answers for you and you'll find that you probably have a million responses.

Be curious and you'll always be learning. When I was younger there were times in my life when I wasn't sure how to talk to people. I didn't know what to say, didn't think I had anything worth talking about. I finally realized that it wasn't about me, that in fact I could learn more about myself by asking people about themselves.

I've been deeply grateful for the friendships I've formed in my life. I think my mother taught me how to do this, how to sustain lasting relationships. She was a wonderful friend to the people in her life, forging long friendships with many women, and devoting herself to them in times of need and in times of leisure.

I think I'm teaching you girls these same values. Our

## After This

days are full of friends. Vera, often in the mornings you'll ask me, "Who's coming over today?" and usually there is someone. The women in my life are important to me. They sustain me in ways that would be impossible for anyone else to.

Relationships are tricky, though. There is a great push and pull, a giving and a receiving, and a balance that must be sought. You will have so many relationships in your life. Friends will come and go; romantic partners will run the gamut from those who rip you apart to those who fill you up.

Always have a center you can return to. A center within yourselves, and one within a circle of people whom you love and trust. Our friends are our chosen family, but we must choose them wisely. Choose people who deeply understand you, who enhance you, not deplete you.

Often we look to others for what we cannot find in ourselves, but this can be a double-edged sword. Sometimes it's true that we can find what we are lacking in another person. There will be people who make you feel complete. But sometimes when we look to someone else to complete us, it is a mistake, and the real work lies in completing ourselves first. My mother once wrote to me, "Find yourself and you'll find your other self."

Above all, be generous with the people in your life. Give your love and trust and support, give your material possessions and your time and your listening ear, and you will receive the same in return.

But always remember that you are worthy of only the best kind of love. I've fallen so deeply for friends and romantic partners most often in times when I was weak and not able to give myself what I needed in the first place. But in the times when I've been hurt by those relationships I've only grown stronger in repairing the damage.

Don't be afraid to be vulnerable, to open yourself up to love. Don't be afraid to receive love. When we close ourselves off we just end up closing off the whole world. Remember that if you get hurt, you will just grow stronger as you heal.

> With love from an open, bleeding heart,
>
> *Mama*

# Chapter Nine

Finally the night comes when my older daughter, Vera, asks *where* my parents are. Now almost five years old, she has asked a lot of questions about how they died, but until now she has taken my answers about their illnesses and eventual deaths at face value. She has simply accepted that they are gone and they are not coming back.

But one evening she asks me what happened to them when they died. This is the question I've been dreading, the question I've been trying to find an answer to myself.

"Well, sweetie," I say, drawing out my words, trying to buy time as various answers swirl through my head.

Vera and I recently read Maria Shriver's *What's Heaven?*, a children's book about death, and I liked the way she explained the concept of the soul.

"Vera, remember when we talked about what the soul is? That it's, like, all the parts that make up who you are? The love you have for me and Dad and your sister, your friendships, and all of your favorite things? Well," I continued, speaking slowly, "when you die, all of those things are still real, but you're not in your body anymore."

"But what happens to your body?" she asks, looking up at me with her big blue eyes.

I take a deep breath. "Well, it stops working and it begins to disintegrate, just like those bananas we didn't finish last week, or the flowers that are wilting on the dining room table right now."

I'm worried that this explanation is going to be frightening, and I have a memory of lying in bed with my own mother when I was about Vera's age, around the same time I began to learn about death. I had developed the irrational fear that my heart would stop, and as I lay there in the dark with my mother, I kept whispering to her that I couldn't feel my heart beating and that I was worried that it wasn't anymore.

"No, sweetie," she murmured to me. "Your heart is beating just fine. You don't have to worry about it."

But I did. I worried that at any moment it would all just stop. That my body would stop working. That life itself would stop. Remembering this, I worry about imparting those same fears to Vera.

I watch her look over at the flowers on the dining room table, wondering if she is recalling the partially brown banana she turned her nose up at before I threw it into the garbage can the other day. I have the impulse to keep explaining, to offer her comfort, but I suddenly feel compelled to wait. It's the same impulse I fight in sessions with my clients when I see them struggling through something. Over the years I've found that if I just wait, they usually come to a profound question or realization on their own, one that I would have interrupted had I been quick to offer comfort in the face of their unease.

"What happened to your parents' bodies after they died?" Vera finally asks after a moment. "Like, what did you do with them?"

"Well," I say slowly, "you can do two things with someone's body after they die." Again, I hesitate. I know that what I am about to say could sound frightening.

## After This

"What kind of things?" Vera asks immediately, eager to hear more.

"After someone dies," I begin, "you either bury them in the ground in a cemetery so that their body can become part of the earth again, or you have them cremated and you scatter their ashes somewhere."

"What's 'cremated'?" Vera asks, and again I take a deep breath.

"Cremation is when you burn the body and turn it into ash. That's what we did with my parents. I still have their ashes. And I take them to different places sometimes and scatter them."

Vera looks perplexed. "What's ashes? Can I see them?"

It's past seven at night. Juliette is asleep, and Vera and I are alone in the living room. Should I show her my parents' ashes? I look at her carefully. She looks back at me with a steady, curious gaze.

Finally I push my way up and head to the hall closet, where there are two bags containing my parents' ashes, hidden away behind towels and extra blankets. My father took a very casual approach to acknowledging this stark truth about death, and it allowed me to relax enough about it myself to keep a collection of ashes in my linen closet at age thirty-five.

When my mother died, my father had her cremated, and then he proceeded to scatter her ashes around various places in the world that had been meaningful to her. The first time I caught him using a salad-serving spoon to transfer some of her ashes into a Ziploc bag so that he could take them to the beach where they had gotten engaged, I was profoundly disturbed.

He was making the transfer between the two bags in the trunk of his car in the driveway of my aunt's house on Cape Cod, and I remember watching with horror as a gust of wind blew the top layer of ash off the spoon as he moved to pour them into the Ziploc.

"Dad!" I exclaimed. "What are you doing?"

I remember the way he sighed, pausing in his endeavor and leaving the serving spoon sticking out of the bag of ashes, as he leaned against the side of the car to address me. "Honey, this is just life. It's not always easy, but it doesn't have to be terrible either."

He gestured to the ashes. "This doesn't have to be a big deal. Let's just take these up to Nauset Beach, okay?"

I stared at him for a moment, processing his attitude, his calmness about the whole thing. He was right, I realized. I could balk at this. I could cry and rage and run away. Or I could just help my father finish transferring the ashes and get in the car with him and drive to the beach. So that's what I did, and when I did it, I knew that it was easier than fighting it all.

So I decide to take the same attitude with Vera. I pull out the bag of ashes from the closet as she sits at the dining room table, watching me eagerly. The large bag is made of dark blue velvet, and I place it on the table before her, opening it up. Inside are two heavy plastic bags—one with my mother's ashes; one with my father's. I remove them from the velvet bag and set them down before her.

"These are their ashes," I say, pointing to each bag. My mother's ashes are dark in color, with small fragments that must be bone scattered within the dust. My father's are a pale white and finer in texture. I watch Vera inspect the contents.

"Why are they different colors?" Vera asks.

"I'm not sure," I say, because truthfully I have no idea.

"Can I touch them?" she asks, peering down into the bag.

Something in me hesitates at her request, but I recognize it as the same feeling I had when I saw my father with the serving spoon. I think to myself then, *Why not? Why not let her touch them? This is life. This is death.*

"Okay," I say, opening the bag of my mother's ashes a bit wider.

Vera reaches into the bag and skims the surface of the ashes with one finger. She lifts it up, studying her fingertip, which is now covered in a fine layer of the powdery fragments.

"I've been taking the ashes to different places for many years," I tell her. "My dad and I took some of my mother's to the beach where they got engaged. And we took some of her ashes to her father's grave in a cemetery. I even took some of them to Italy, a place she really loved. And when my dad died I took some of his ashes to the same beach where we took my mother's. I also took some to Michigan, where he was born. I put them in a lake there that he used to swim in as a kid."

Vera is still looking at the ash on her finger.

"How do you make ash?" she asks, uninterested in my description of what I've done with them.

"Well, you have to burn something with fire, and then it becomes ash."

She just stares at me blankly.

"Here, let me show you," I say, and together we get up from the dining room table and go into the kitchen. I grab a piece of paper from a drawer, and a packet of matches. We stand at the kitchen sink and I light the match, gently touching it to the paper. We watch the flame consume the paper, and then as little flakes of ash float down into the sink basin. I touch my finger to a piece of ash and hold it up to Vera.

"See?" I say. "Just like that."

"Cool," she says, looking at the ash on both of our fingers. I study her face, trying to figure out what's going through her mind, worrying that this is all too much.

"Can we burn something else?" she asks then, with a mischievous smile on her face.

I just laugh, and something in me relaxes. I've been being so careful, so gentle with this whole experience, coming at it from the very adult perspective I have, but in this moment I see it all from her point of view.

It *is* cool, I realize. Life and death and transformation. It's all so strange and beautiful and magical, and also so simple.

"Not tonight, sweetie," I say with a smile. "But sure, we'll do it again soon."

"Okay, Mama," she says, just like she always does when she's satisfied with something.

A few weeks later I go to Bali to visit Cat. My husband and I have recently separated, and he's taken our daughters to visit his family in Ohio. Rather than spend a week in my empty house in Los Angeles, I decide to head to the bastion of newly divorced women who are trying to find answers in their lives. Really, I'm just going to see my friend, but the moment I set foot in Ubud I'm painfully aware of each lost-seeming woman who walks by with a guidebook in her hand.

I've been thinking a lot about the experiences I've had over the past several years, the mediums and rabbis, the past-life regressions and shaman circles. I feel I could spend the rest of my life searching for answers to the question of what happens when we die. I've considered traveling to India, to the places that were so transformative to my friend Julie. I want to see the bodies being burned on the Ganges. I want to gaze at the Taj Mahal and contemplate the meaning of existence.

I want to go to an African funeral and witness their ancient burial rites. I want to trek through the Peruvian rain forest and take ayahuasca under the stars with an old shaman. I want to visit Mayan temples, and I want to sit in meditation with monks in Nepal. I want to talk to physicists and I want to attend this monthly meeting of near-death-experience survivors in Los Angeles I've heard about.

## After This

But the thing is that I'm a thirty-five-year-old mother of two with a busy life and career. I've got a house to take care of, clients to see, bills to pay, weekly trips to Target to contend with.

I've got to live life, not death.

So instead I go to Bali to visit Cat, so that I don't have to face the sadness of being alone in my house without my children.

Cat and I met on an airplane on the Fourth of July one year. I was on my way from Los Angeles to Boston. I had only recently met the man who would become my husband, the very man I have so recently separated from, and he was meeting me on Cape Cod so I could introduce him to my extended family. As I stood waiting to board the plane that day, I had the sense that everything in my life was reaching some glimmering peak. For weeks each day had felt portentous, and I looked around the terminal that morning, wondering whom I would sit next to on the plane. I couldn't explain why, but I knew that it would be someone who would become important in my life.

The boarding call came and I slung my bag over my shoulder and walked down the gangway. My father had been dead for four years; my mother, for eleven. I had boarded hundreds of flights in their absence, the feeling of flinging myself out into some part of the world always acting as a temporary balm for the wildness that roiled inside me, and as I stepped onto this plane, the familiar feeling of a weight being lifted rose through me.

I took my seat at the window and removed a book and a journal from my bag. It was 2007 and I was, along with every other woman in the world, reading *Eat, Pray, Love*. The plane slowly filled up, but the two seats next to me remained open. I had begun to think that no one would be sitting next to me after all, when a young woman with wild hair and warm green eyes walked onto the plane and took the seat next to the aisle in our row, leaving the middle seat between us empty. We smiled at each other and then I went back to writing in my journal.

I paused during takeoff, leaning my forehead against the tiny airplane window as Los Angeles receded below us. There's something magical about taking off from LAX. No matter where you're headed, you take off over the Pacific Ocean, heading west toward the horizon. Just before you start to panic, thinking, *Wait, Boston lies in the opposite direction*, wondering if you've gotten on the wrong flight, the plane banks and arcs back over the coast, heading east, the tiniest feeling of disappointment pinging through you as you realize that maybe you aren't accidentally headed to some exotic locale after all.

After my plane to Boston leveled off, I looked back to see that the young woman next to me was writing in a journal as well. I finished my entry, closed the cover of my notebook, and my eyes, and drifted off into that weird airplane sleep. After an hour or so I woke up. My seatmate had also been asleep. Her eyes were closed, and I took in her hippie garb, a faded paisley tank top and a long flowy skirt, beaded bracelets encircling her wrists. Her eyes blinked open suddenly as I was watching her, and I quickly turned my gaze away.

"I just had a dream about you," she said, reaching out to touch my arm. "We were little children in India, sisters," she continued. "It was so strange. It was so real, unlike anything I can explain."

My only response was to laugh, and then she laughed too.

"God, you probably think I'm crazy," she said.

"Not at all. I'm Claire, by the way," I said, introducing myself.

She laughed and extended her hand. "I'm Cat."

We spent the rest of the flight laughing and talking. Cat was fresh off a flight from Bali, where she lived and worked as a yoga instructor. She was on her way to Boston, where her father lived. We talked all through the rest of the flight, and exchanged contact information before the plane landed. Over the next seven years we fostered our friendship, despite the distance.

In a weird coincidence, her father moved to Chicago that summer, the same month I moved there to be with my husband. Every few months Cat would come through town and we would spend an evening together, talking about life in a way that I hadn't done with someone since Julie died. Cat was deeply spiritual, but also funny and grounded and real. She'd had a hard adolescence riddled with various traumas, and it had caused her to ask a lot of the same big questions I always found myself asking.

One night we sat out on the deck at my apartment in Chicago talking about death. I had just begun to formulate my intentions to write this book and I wanted to know what Cat thought about death. She was full of interesting stories and ideas, but the one we mutually settled on that night was one that would linger for me.

Our talk about death had led us to the opposite—to talking about life, and about all the different choices we make as humans. I sat up in my seat suddenly, the warm evening air bathing us in comfort.

"What if there are as many ways to be dead as there are to be alive?" I proposed. "Like, what if whatever you believe now is what you get? Like, if you believe in a puffy white heaven or a fiery hell, or a blank nothingness, then that is what you'll find when you cross over?"

Cat nodded at me enthusiastically. "Yes, yes," she said. "That makes so much sense."

I went to bed that night grateful to have friends with whom I could have these conversations. If death and loss were going to be such big parts of my life I wanted to be able to talk about them.

When Cat greets me at the airport in Bali we just laugh when we see each other. In all the years I've known her she's always been the one to visit me, and I'm excited to see her world. It's late at night when I arrive, and we immediately climb into a car that will drive us north, into the mountains, where we'll spend a few days at a hot springs resort relaxing and catching up.

Cat tells me about Balinese culture as we wind along the narrow roads heading north.

"Why does everyone say it's so magical here?" I ask.

"Because of all the ceremonies," she explains. "The Balinese are very superstitious and they have this deep reverence for spirits. They're always honoring them, holding all kinds of ceremonies all the time to appease the spirits. The spirits know this, so there are more of them here than anywhere else."

"Hmm," I say in response, glancing out the window at the dark trees floating past, thinking about how little attention is paid to ritual and ceremony in my regular life.

That first night at the resort I can't sleep. The breeze pushes through the screens and my feet keep getting tangled in the mosquito netting over the bed. At one point I dream that a large spirit is trying to get into our room, and I'm immediately awakened by the door slamming open. I get up and close it, glancing back to the bed where Cat is still asleep.

I tell her about the dream and the door the next morning over breakfast and she immediately asks our Balinese waiter if there are many spirits at the resort.

"Oh, yes," he replies gravely. "What room are you in?"

Cat tells him which room we have and about my dream and the door. His eyes grow wide. "That's exactly where the big spirits are here at the resort, at the edge of the property next to your room," he says. Cat just nods and I pause, a piece of mango halfway to my mouth.

"Do you really think it's true?" I ask her.

"Oh, sure," she says casually. "You wouldn't believe what the spirits are capable of."

## After This

I stare out at the water, wondering if a spirit tried to come into our room last night. I don't really believe it, but either way, I like that everyone is so accepting of the idea. Back home this kind of stuff would be whispered and laughed nervously about.

A few days later, back in Ubud, I meet with a friend of Cat's, an intuitive named Paula. We sit on the grassy lawn outside the Yoga Barn, where Cat is an instructor, and Paula arranges herself cross-legged, closing her eyes for a moment. She's young, in her midthirties, and beautiful.

I've met with so many psychics and intuitives at this point that I'm already relaxed. I'm mostly just curious as to her approach and what she'll have to tell me. As per usual, I've told her nothing about me so far, and requested Cat do the same.

After a moment Paula opens her eyes and looks at me. "You do have children? You don't have children? I'm getting such a funny energy about it."

I smile at her, waiting to see what else she comes up with before I give her the answer.

She closes her eyes again. "You do have children," she murmurs. "Girls. They're young. But you're not held down by them the way most mothers are."

I nod at her, and let her keep talking. I'm interested in this notion that I'm not held down by my children.

"I'm not saying you're not a devoted mother," she says. "I'm definitely getting that you are, but you're not confined by motherhood; that's what I'm saying."

"I suppose so," I say. "I mean, I'm here in Bali without them."

Paula nods and pulls out a deck of tarot cards, handing them to me to shuffle. When I'm done she begins to lay them out one by one in some kind of order.

She tells me various things about my life that ring true: that I work in a helping profession, that I value communication and use it in my work. She tells me the same thing that Gahl, the astrologer, told me, that I come from a long line of psychics and mystics, that I was perhaps a witch in another life.

"You've got all that stuff now," Paula says, referring to my potential psychic abilities, "but you're more grounded in this life. You want to communicate this stuff but not in some hippie Burning Man way. You want to make what's normally taboo accessible, to just make it part of real life."

"Exactly," I tell her. And it's true. That's been my whole mission behind exploring the afterlife. There are so many books out there about what happens when we die, but so often they're written by psychics and mediums, or they're scholarly and academic. How does a person lead a regular life and still find some connection to what happens next? That's what I'm trying to figure out.

"Your mother passed," Paula says then, and I nod. I'm no longer surprised when the psychics I meet come up with this stuff. I've actually come to expect it.

"She's actually been here the whole time," she says about my mother. "You were young, a teenager. It feels like she went at a crucial time in your world. You felt you didn't know what to do without her, even though you did."

This is all true. In some ways, I still feel lost without her.

"When someone passes," Paula explains, "an energy is created around that moment, and it lives. They've showed me this, my guides. The energy created depends on the intensity of the connection, and in this case with your mother, I feel it was quite big."

That sounds like an understatement to me. My mother's death was the defining moment of my life. Everything about who I am today is because of her death.

"We have to learn how to deal with this energy when it is created.

## After This

Some people stuff it down," Paula says. "But it has to manifest. If we push it down it can become disease and disrupt our lives. Or we can surrender to it and let it integrate as part of our experience."

I think about this, and about my work with the shamans last year, about that piece of my soul that I lost. This idea seems to parallel Paula's explanation about energy being created.

"You have to remember that you wouldn't be doing half of what you're doing had she not died. And she is with you. She is fully with you on the other side. That was always the deal. She's writing with you. She's giving you inspiration. She has a very, very strong energy in your life."

Later, after my session, I wonder to myself if perhaps this is all the afterlife is, the swirling energy and ramifications of losing someone—all the ways those of us who are left behind change, the actions we take, the pursuits we embark on, the ways we change the world as a result.

On my second-to-last day in Bali—New Year's Eve there—Cat and I go to see a Balinese water priestess. It's a hot and humid day and we hire a driver to take us way out into the countryside to the temple where the priestess resides.

As we bump and twist along the dirt roads, I lean my head against the window, watching the streets stream by, banana trees and old women carrying baskets on their heads, mangy dogs and motorbikes parked askew. Fireworks go off intermittently (they've been going off for days) and that eighties song "Forever Young" plays on the car radio (it will be stuck in my head for weeks).

After an hour or so, we finally arrive at the temple. It isn't what I was expecting. I've been picturing a forest temple like something out of a Peter Jackson film, lush and green, a waterfall, maybe, dripping flowers and an incandescent quality to the air. But instead the driver parks outside a crumbling concrete wall on a dilapidated roadside and waves his hand toward a simple doorway.

Cat and I gather our things and make our way inside, past a statue adorned with flowers and offerings, and onto the grounds of an old temple that is, for the most part, under construction. Workers are laying bricks and flies buzz about; an old dog limps by. We make our way toward the back of the grounds, past a fountain and a little house, to a kind of pavilion set against the lush trees I imagined.

We sit on simple mats to wait for the priestess, and I watch a caterpillar crawl by. I am exhausted, weary from travel and emotion. I look over at Cat and she smiles at me, that warm, familiar smile I've grown to know so well over the past seven years.

As we wait for the water priestess to arrive this is what I'm thinking about. All these years of knowing Cat, and I'm finally here in Bali with her. I smile at her again and her eyes crinkle in response. We have the kind of friendship in which most of the time we can't stop talking, yet there are also moments when we have to say nothing at all to know what the other is thinking.

I'm glad I'm here, but I'm exhausted. The heat is making me dizzy and it seems like forever before the priestess finally emerges from her temple to climb the stairs, taking a seat across from us.

She folds her hands in her lap and looks at both of us, squaring her face to ours. She is young, in her late twenties, but her eyes are stern, her countenance unforgiving. Again, I don't know what to expect. Cat didn't explain much, and the priestess didn't either. That has been the theme of the trip thus far anyway—just showing up and opening myself to whatever the experience has to offer.

"We are going to meditate now for forty-five minutes," the priestess says, and immediately a stillness goes through her. I shift my position, trying to find some pose that will sustain me for that period of

## After This

time, but I am already restless and tired of the heat. I close my eyes anyway and take a deep breath, and I can sense Cat doing the same beside me.

After all these years of practicing meditation I've developed a real awe and wonder for the moments when I can achieve that space between my thoughts. It has not come easy for me, but in the instances when everything truly does go still amid the usual swirling of all the things I think make up who I am, I am left with a peace I didn't know was possible, one that sometimes becomes just an idea later, of something I might have someday in a more lasting way.

I search for it then, for that space, that quiet, sitting there under the pavilion next to my friend, and across from this strange young priestess, but all I can think about are the past twelve months of my life.

Since moving back to Los Angeles from Chicago I have become lost in marriage and motherhood. After the birth of my second daughter I felt as though I was drowning. My husband and I flailed about to stay afloat in our lives, struggling financially and with our careers. We have reached a place that seems like an impasse. The fact that he is in Ohio with our children and I am in Bali is symbolic of the vast distance that has come between us.

I sit in the heat with my eyes closed, trying to find stillness, but after a while I give up entirely on pushing everything out of my head and I let the thoughts run freely.

Cicadas hum in the trees around me and I feel a drip of sweat slide down the small of my back. I shift in my seat, my palms open to the warm air, and in my head I chastise myself for these thoughts. I am in Bali, for chrissake, meeting with a water priestess. I am supposed to be finding some kind of divine meditation, and instead, all I can think about is everything in my life that I'm doing wrong.

I try finding the stillness again. It really exists, this place between all the thoughts. It's serene there, and I long for it. But the images continue to flood through me, a whole kaleidoscope of my past year, a thousand memories and moments and sensations. It crashes through me, my cells alight with pure memory, a cascading sense of love and loss, of failure and repartition.

Tears are streaming down my cheeks by the time the priestess begins to call a long, low song, breaking us from our meditation. I've lost sense of time, of my body, of any purpose I had in this visit. I open my eyes slowly and find the priestess watching me. She nods approvingly at my tears, and motions for us to stand. Cat smiles at me and I don't bother to wipe the tears from my cheeks; instead I just push to my feet and follow them to another part of the grounds.

It is midday by now, the sun beating down in a punishing swath of liquid gold. My sarong clings to the backs of my legs and I haven't showered in days. We enter another outdoor temple, a confusing amalgam of statues and stairways. The priestess points to a hard, concrete ledge that protrudes from beneath the wall, a spot laid bare in the harsh noon sun, and tells us to sit. We will meditate for an hour this time, she says.

I look at Cat, my mouth agape. Can I withstand this? It surely seems like some form of punishment, of torture. The tears on my face are drying quickly in the heat and I run a hand through my hair, again a sense of giving myself over to it all flowing through me. I take a seat, pull my knees to my chest, and watch the priestess ascend a covered altar that faces us some distance away. A dog pads into the compound, plopping down beside me, its tongue lolling with drool from the side of its mouth. A fly buzzes in my ear, and again I close my eyes.

I give up on the stillness altogether; my only mission is to make my way through this next hour with whatever grace I have left. The priestess begins to chant, a low, guttural moaning that becomes the

## After This

only thing I focus on. There is nothing else. The memories, the fear, the sadness—it is all gone.

My body becomes slick with sweat and I can no longer sense the dog beside me. From time to time I let my eyes slit open, but the light is so bright that I quickly pinch them shut again, disappearing into the priestess's chanting. After a while she begins to ring a bell, a continuous sound that chimes along with her voice until they are seemingly one. My father is there then, not really thoughts of him, but more of a general sense of his love for me. I feel my head slip and I shift position, losing consciousness altogether.

When I come to it's as though I have been dropped into my body anew. My limbs are rubbery foreign things and I fit myself into them with wonder. This is where I live? This is the body I inhabit? The life I lead? It seems both enchanting and meaningless.

There are other moments too, other thoughts and revelations, a visit from Julie, who laughs at the sight of me and Cat sitting there in the sun in this countryside temple. I can see us from her vantage point, these two unlikely friends, bound like sisters from lifetimes past.

I don't know how it ends, exactly. I only feel the sensation of pushing my way to standing, of crossing the floor of the temple to stand beneath the altar, the priestess smiling down at us, her eyes tight. We stand to the side while three Balinese women, one holding a strange bald baby, take their place before the priestess, who begins her chanting again, while she pours water from a long-handled wooden bucket over their heads.

The women stamp their feet and moan, the water splashing to the ground around them, drenching their clothes and washing through their hair. They run their hands across their faces, lifting the water to their mouths, taking it in, seemingly begging for more. The baby is crying, reaching for its mama, who stands some distance away, and I watch all this, thinking about what that water will feel like when it is my turn.

Finally the women depart and the priestess motions for Cat and me to stand before her. We take our places beneath the altar, and again, the priestess looks down at me with discerning eyes. She nods at a young girl beside her, who submerges the handled bucket in the water, passing it to the priestess, who holds it above my head.

I long for the water. I imagine how cool and refreshing it will feel, the cleanse and release that will surely come.

But it isn't like that.

The water is harsh, cascading over me in such a torrential way that I cannot breathe. Over and over she pours and I gasp for air, trying to run my hands across my face and through my hair as the Balinese women did, but I can only clamor for oxygen, my heart pounding, sobs escaping between my sputtering, panicked breaths. The priestess seems to delight in my misery, and again this feels like punishment, a deserved one.

I realize in this moment that all my life I've felt that I deserve to be punished, for wanting so much, for taking so much from this world, from the people who love me. The water crashes down over me and it isn't just the priestess's delight I feel, but the delight of all those whom I have hurt—my children, my friends, my family. I can feel them all smiling, nodding at me, in that moment.

*Yes, this is what she deserves*, they seem to be saying.

*Yes, this is what I deserve*, I think to myself.

The priestess is telling me to let it out, to stomp my feet, to moan and release, but I can only shake and hold myself tighter, still gasping for air and space and breath, knowing that this is surely the only way I can spend the last day of 2013.

When it is finally over I run my fingers through my hair and step aside, my clothing clinging to my narrow frame, all notions of who

## After This

I was going into this experience like some leftover memory from a long time ago. The feeling is the same as the one that comes in savasana, at the end of yoga. It is the same as the eventual stillness I've found in other meditation experiences, one of rest, of surrender to what is.

When I get home from Bali I clear off a small hutch in my dining room that once held a few framed photographs and a messy bowl full of keys and pens and things. I dig out of storage a tiny hand-carved wooden table that Julie once sent me after a trip to India and I place it there on the hutch, along with a few figurines I purchased in Bali. I add several candles, and a bowl of seashells from the beach where my parents got engaged. After that I find some rocks I've picked up in places like Sedona and Big Sur, and I search for a tiny bear figurine I bought before leaving the shaman workshops in Bozeman.

I arrange everything on the hutch that first week back from Bali, and one night I stand before it all and light the candles. I close my eyes and I think about my parents, and about Julie. I think about all the journeys I've taken over the past few years in an effort to glean a better understanding of what life and death are about. I'm not really meditating, and I'm not really praying either. I'm just standing there, trying to be present and to let myself feel everything, all the love and the pain and the future and the past, and my bare feet on the floor of my dining room in this very moment.

Everything about this ritual feels both unfamiliar and inherently natural. I wonder to myself why I haven't been doing this sort of thing my whole life, taking these moments of surrender and presence, moments of reflection and honor.

I begin lighting the candles all the time. I light them when I'm feeling sad or worried about something, and during times when I'm jubilant and optimistic about the future. I think about different things when I stand there before my little altar, but always I picture my parents there, standing behind me. Julie too. I let myself feel them, their love for me and my love for them. It's a love that is real, no matter where they are now.

My daughters are fascinated with the table. They stand before it too, touching the various items on it and sometimes moving things around or adding tiny toys of their own. I don't mind. One of the things that Paula, the intuitive in Bali, told me was that I had to be sure to teach my daughters a reverence for the mystical, and after my talks with Vera over the past year, I feel more of a desire than ever to give her some sense of the magic we can't quite see in life.

This idea of ritual nags at me, and I begin to ask my clients about their own sense of it, encouraging them to bring it into their lives more. I know that for some people praying and going to church provide this, but for those of us without a religious foundation, we may be lacking the important act of ritual in our lives.

I think about how in Bali shopkeepers hold tiny ceremonies before the start of each day, just before they open their shops, and how most Balinese make general offerings to the gods at the start and close of each day. There are ceremonies for new babies, and ceremonies for deaths. There are offerings made when they dream of dead loved ones, or sometimes just when they are thinking of them.

There is a beauty in this that adds a sense of peace to our lives and our grief. In our culture we so often strive to move past the loss, but I think that rather than moving past it, finding a way to incorporate it into our lives makes more sense.

We don't have to follow strict rituals like the ones in Bali, with their hand gestures and offerings of fruit and flowers. Doing what feels right to us is all that matters. Simply placing a candle before a photo of our loved ones and taking moments here and there to stop

## After This

and honor the relationship and all that it has brought into our lives can be profoundly healing.

Sometimes we get so caught up in cultural or religious ideas of how we're supposed to do things that we forget how powerful it can be to simply make up our own rituals and ceremonies. And I don't think we should be afraid to share these things with our children. Just as we may have changed our beliefs about certain doctrines that we were exposed to as a child, they will also one day take what they want from whatever ideas we offer them.

I think we need to remember that when we're talking to children about death it's okay not to have all the answers. We can ask them what *they* think happens when we get stumped by one of their questions, or tell them about the various explanations we've heard about for the questions they have. Simply creating space and allowing them to talk about these things is the healthiest route.

We can involve them in our rituals and ceremonies and customs, and ask them to participate and add their own creative ideas to whatever it is we're doing. I'm often surprised by the sweet and delightful additions they come up with. Children internalize the concept of love in a much more simple way than adults do, and listening to their ideas can remind us of the foundation of what it means to care for someone.

---

On my mother's birthday, in March, I ask the girls to join me in front of the table. "Today is my mother's birthday," I tell them.

Vera perks up. "We should make her a cake!" she exclaims.

"We should," I say with a laugh. "But first I want to light some candles for her."

"Okay." Vera nods, as though we have done this a hundred times before.

I strike a match and let Vera touch the flame to the wicks of the candles. She does so reverently, and I watch the flames take hold.

"Next, let's all hold hands and close our eyes," I say. The girls stand on either side of me and take each of my hands. Their warm little fingers wrap around mine and I close my eyes. "Let's think about my mother now," I say, "and let's send her love, and let ourselves feel her love."

"Oh, like when I send you messages in my head?" Vera asks.

"Yes, exactly like that," I reply.

"She'll be able to hear us, just like you can hear me," Vera says without an ounce of disbelief.

"I think she will," I say.

So we stand there and close our eyes, the three of us, all of us a result of the woman who gave birth to me, and the women who came before her.

When we're done we go into the kitchen to make a cake. "We have to sing 'Happy Birthday' to her when we're done," Vera says.

I nod. "Yes, let's do it."

"But I get to blow out the candles because I'm the oldest, and because I look like her," Vera adds.

"Sure," I say with a laugh, and I begin taking ingredients out of the cupboard.

This is the afterlife, I think. My two daughters and I, baking a cake in the kitchen just as I used to do with my own mother, all of us bound together by blood and life and death and love.

## After This

Dear Vera and Jules,

Last week I took you for a checkup at the doctor's office and you both got a few shots. Picture me sitting on the exam table, one of you in each of my arms, clinging to me, hot and sweaty with tears and quaking sobs. My heart both breaks and swells into a million pieces in those moments, so strong is the love I have for you.

Afterward, Vera, I told you that you were very brave.

"No, Mommy," you replied. "I wasn't brave because I was scared."

"But that's exactly what being brave is," I explained. "Doing something, even when you're afraid."

You didn't reply, just nodded solemnly and stared out the window, thinking about what I'd said.

I've been thinking about it too. I'd never quite put it into words like that before, this thing called bravery.

The truth is that I'm afraid all the time. I'm scared of everything.

I'm afraid that I'm not a good enough mother, that there are a thousand missteps I'm making along our way. I'm afraid that I won't be able to do all the things I want to do, write the books I envision, get to all the places I want to go. I'm scared that I'm not a good enough friend, that I fail to put others before myself. I fear for my work and my housekeeping abilities.

I'm afraid of being alone. I'm scared that I'll be lonely again one day. I worry about my health and my culinary abilities. I'm afraid of hurting people, of not being in the places I'm supposed to be. I'm afraid of being judged, and I'm afraid of judging others. I worry sometimes that the words I write aren't as real as they could be. Sometimes I realize I'm not breathing, and I'm afraid that one day I'll stop altogether.

Yet.

Despite all of those swirling anxieties, I get up every day and plunge forth, wading through the thickness of my life, leaning into it all as though there is no other choice.

So, by my own definition, is that bravery? Living my life, even though I'm afraid to?

I think about the day I sold my second book, the very one that this letter will be in. It was a profound moment in my life. Vera, you were at school, and Jules, you were taking a nap, when the call came in from my agent that Penguin had made an offer. I hung up the phone and wept for a solid twenty minutes.

I just stood in the living room by myself in the middle of the day, looking around and weeping. All I've ever wanted since I was a little girl was to write books, to be a real author, and something about selling my second book confirmed that dream as a reality.

I also wept that my parents are not here to witness my accomplishments, the taste of that desire as bittersweet as you can imagine. And then I wiped my face, woke you, Jules, with a hundred kisses, and picked up you, Vera, from school, and swept you both off to the beach, where the world is wide and wonderful and real.

I've been traveling a lot this past year, leaving you both in the care of your doting father while I head out into

## After This

the world. It's felt amazing to be alone. To be quiet, to be unsure, and to be lonely and scared. To be in a hotel room in a strange city, tucked into a big bed, all by myself. To wake up in the morning and speak to no one for the first couple of hours, all of it the very opposite of motherhood.

I've missed you immensely on those days, in those places, but I've also gulped down those solitary moments, drinking in as much as I can before returning to our life together. These days have been important to me, and I have this funny feeling that they'll be important to you as well—not just when you have these same experiences, but when you find out that your mother did.

There's nothing quite like traveling alone. It requires bravery. Stepping off an airplane in a foreign city, renting a car and driving down a road you've never known, eating dinner alone in a restaurant, putting yourself to bed at night, only to wake early so that you can hike through an unfamiliar forest, the only sound your own footsteps.

If there's ever a moment in your lives when you're feeling unsure of who you are, take a little journey, step into an unfamiliar place, and you'll remember who you are.

I think that's one of the bravest things you can really do in life. Remember who you are.

Love from everywhere,

*Mama*

## Chapter Ten

It's a Monday morning in early August and I am sitting in the office of psychic medium Fleur, on the west side of Los Angeles. I know this will be my last visit to a medium for a while. I've seen enough of them now that my curiosity has been quelled, and I'm satisfied that this has been a rewarding experience. However, there is one last person I'm hoping to hear from.

I made this appointment after learning that my friend Abby, who died just two months ago, came through to another friend during a recent reading she attended with Fleur. Of all the people I've lost in my life already, Abby's death has been one of the hardest to contend with. A thirty-seven-year-old married mother of two young children, Abby had been one of my closest friends for all of my adult life. Watching her succumb to breast cancer and say good-bye to her little family has rocked me.

I need to know that she is okay.

Fleur takes a seat opposite me and smiles brightly. She is young and pretty, in her midtwenties, and I wonder about her life path briefly while she gets settled. She looks like someone I'd be friends with. She's wearing cute shoes and lip gloss. I can imagine us shopping or having lunch together. How is it that she can speak to the dead and I cannot?

She closes her eyes for a moment. "There are several people already here for you," she says.

"Yes, I invited quite a few," I admit.

Last night I closed my eyes in bed and talked in my head to all those I was hoping might come through. *Hi Mom, hi Dad, Julie, Abby. I'm going to see a medium named Fleur in the Howard Hughes office building in West LA tomorrow. I would love it if you wanted to come and talk to me.* It's funny to me how doing something like this seems so normal at this point.

My mother and father come through to Fleur straightaway. I've told her nothing about myself, and she's requested that I do not give her any information during the reading, that I tell her only if the information she is conveying to me is correct. She describes the illnesses my parents died from, their ages, my age at the times of their deaths. Everything she tells me is accurate.

She tells me that my mother's mother is passed as well, and that they are together on the other side, that my mother's sister is with her as well. I nod, validating that my grandmother and my aunt are both dead. Fleur tells me that my father's parents are gone too, that they died when I was young and that I didn't know them very well (also accurate), but that my father is with them and they are all watching from the other side.

"Your mom is sorry that she didn't prepare you more for her death," Fleur tells me then. "She wishes that she had put more things, more people in place, to support you after she was gone. She's sorry that you were on your own the way you were."

I nod. I've heard these same sentiments from my mother through the other mediums I've visited. It's nice to hear, in a way—just that recognition from her, from anyone, that this has been hard on me.

## After This

"She keeps expressing something about three. Three females," Fleur says.

"She had three sisters," I reply.

"Maybe," Fleur says, "but I don't think that's it. Are you a mother?"

"I am. I have two little girls."

"Yes, that's what she's talking about. She's telling me that she's watching over the three of you all the time."

I smile. I think that all I really want to know at this point is that my mom and dad aren't missing all this. I desperately want them to know that I have these two beautiful daughters, that I have become a mother, and that becoming so has been the best part of my life so far.

After a few more accurate details and sweet sentiments from my parents, Fleur tells me that she is going to connect with a couple more people who are waiting to communicate with me.

"I have a young woman here," she says. "She would have died recently, sometime in the last year or so."

I nod, hoping this is Abby.

I met Abby when I was twenty years old; she trained me as a waitress at a busy restaurant in New York's Union Square. It was the same restaurant, in fact, where I was working when my friend Julie became sick with leukemia.

The restaurant, a hip pan-Asian place, was stocked with a glamorous assortment of young waitresses who were learning how to design clothing lines at the Fashion Institute, or others who were trying to make it as actresses. They were young and stunning, and I felt a constant sense of awkwardness around them.

Abby was no exception to this cast of beautiful girls. In fact, she was quite possibly the most beautiful of them all. Perfectly fit, with an athletic build and gorgeous curly hair that fell down her back, she moved through the restaurant turning heads at every table. The way she carried herself made her seem like a goddess, and I marveled at the way someone so young could inhabit so much confidence and beauty.

But what set Abby apart from the other waitresses, who giggled and traded makeup tips together by the service station, was that she was also kind. You could find her just as easily lost in deep philosophical conversation about cultural differences with the crew of Ecuadorian busboys as you could find her cracking jokes with the handsome bartenders.

Those first couple of years working in the restaurant I kept to myself. I got through my busy shifts and then changed quickly to run to my classes at college, or home to my apartment with my boyfriend Colin. On the days that I worked double shifts, I took my breaks in the park across the square, writing long letters to Julie and feeling isolated in my sadness.

Although Abby had always been friendly with me, just as she was with everyone, we didn't begin to form a friendship right away. But then, in the year following Julie's death, Abby and I found ourselves working the same lunch shifts for a period of time.

Initially I couldn't even believe that she was giving me the time of day, but suddenly we were spending our breaks chatting about our lives, our boyfriends, and our future plans. Abby was finishing her BA at NYU, and pursuing a career as an actress. She was from Boston, and she loved to read. We talked about books and started going to lunch together, then shopping. She cooked dinner for me in her apartment in Brooklyn, where she lived with her older sister, and I made it a point to attend every one of her off-off-Broadway shows.

Although we continued to grow closer, I still pondered her affinity for me. Whereas I felt like a broken girl, lost in sadness and confusion about life, Abby walked through the world with abundant love and confidence. She seemingly lacked the barrier that holds most people back from opening themselves up to others, the barrier that seems to prevent people sometimes from freely bestowing love and acceptance on others. She had her insecurities and her sensitivities, but even those didn't stop her from giving of herself in a way that I just wasn't able to do with the people around me.

We both left New York the same year and ended up in Los Angeles. She was waiting tables again and getting acting gigs in various shows. I was working as an editorial assistant at a fancy magazine and taking care of my elderly father on the weekends. Our friendship grew even deeper as we helped each other build Ikea furniture for our apartments and met up over glasses of wine to moan about the challenges of the careers we were pursuing. When I finally worked up the courage to end my troubled relationship with Colin, it was Abby's futon I slept on for a week. She smoothed my hair while I cried and bought me a new toothbrush.

Shortly after that, my father entered hospice care and I moved into his condo to see him through the final days of his life. I was twenty-five and completely overwhelmed by my caregiving role. Abby was one of several friends who drove the forty-five minutes south to Orange County to support me while I supported him. On the second-to-last day of his life she drove down and found me unshowered and shaking at his bedside. I had been sitting vigil for almost forty-eight hours, not having left his side except to use the bathroom. I was determined to be holding his hand when he died.

"Oh, honey," Abby said in a soft voice. "You need a break."

I stared down at my father. He had been unconscious all morning, his breath slow and rasping.

"Why don't you go take a nice, hot shower? Just for a few minutes, at least," she suggested.

I shook my head at her. I didn't want to leave him. I didn't want him to leave me.

"I'll stay right here, and hold his hand. I promise that I'll come get you if anything at all happens," she said, her eyes imploring me to take this moment for myself.

I looked back at her, and knew that there was probably no one else in the world I would have trusted in that moment. "Okay," I said, nodding at her and making her promise again that she would get me the second anything changed.

The shower felt good and I stood, letting the warm water cascade over me, my tears mingling with the soap. My father was going to be gone in perhaps a matter of hours, and I knew then that I would really be on my own. The future felt huge and empty and terrifying. I stayed in the shower longer than I had intended, but as soon as I had a towel wrapped around me, I peeked my head out the door of the bathroom to check on my dad.

The sight was one that never ceases to bring tears to my eyes when I remember it. There was Abby, sitting at my father's bedside, this man she barely knew—I think she'd actually only met him once before he became sick—and she was holding his hand and singing to him in a soft voice. The melody floated down the hallway to me and I knew then that she had given me the gift of a true friend, that she was, in fact, teaching me what it meant to be one.

In the years that followed my father's death Abby and I went on to become even closer friends, seeing each other through more moves, more boyfriends, our weddings, and the births of our children. Even though we were both busy with our little families and our careers, we always found time to meet up for lunch or a walk by the beach, filling each other in on all the latest.

On one of those beach walks, just last year, Abby showed up looking distraught.

## After This

"Claire," she told me, "I have breast cancer."

We were standing on a busy stretch of a path that ran alongside the ocean in Santa Monica. Rollerbladers and bicyclists streamed by us. I burst into tears at her words and we both stopped walking, clinging to each other as we sobbed into each other's shoulders in the bright California morning. Of all the things we had been through together in our long friendship, I did not want this to be one of them.

After her initial cancer diagnosis Abby immediately began to undergo chemotherapy, followed by a mastectomy, then a round of radiation treatment. Her doctor's office was near my home in Santa Monica, and she would stop by for lunch often during those months. I would make quiche and bounce Juliette on my hip, and we would talk about all the things we always talked about. We had been friends for sixteen years.

We had seen one another through so much, and we marveled, as we often did, at the longevity of our friendship, and all that we had been through, except now our conversations included lengthy talks about death.

I often shared with her bits and pieces of this book as I was working on it, telling her about my talks with the rabbi or my shaman workshops. Sometimes she broke down sobbing at my dining room table, devastated by another scan that showed the cancer was not receding. She didn't want to die. She didn't want to let go of the beautiful life she had created for herself, her children, or her loving husband.

I would put my arms around her and let her cry. But I didn't have any answers. I didn't want her to die.

Her cancer was an aggressive one, though, and less than a year after her initial diagnosis, she was at home under hospice care, at the end of her life. She was thirty-seven years old. Her daughter was three and her son was seven. Her husband, parents, brother, and sister had dedicated themselves entirely to her care, and to helping make her comfortable at the end.

On one of my last visits to her I sat on her bed with my arms around her. She was leaning forward, trying to breathe through her cancer-ravaged lungs.

"You know," she said in a whisper, "I don't really have any regrets in life. There were a couple of bad plays I acted in," she said with a weak smile, "but that's really it."

I smiled back at her, remembering those exact plays, which I had gone to see in New York so many years ago.

"You got to experience more goodness in your thirty-seven years than some people do in a lifetime," I said, staring at a picture on her bedside table of a healthy Abby with her little daughter, Julia, wrapped around her. "But I think it was because you gave so much in return," I told her. "You knew some secret right from the start, a secret that takes most of us our whole lives to learn. You knew that the only thing really worth doing in this life is giving love to everyone around you."

In that moment I thought about what Rabbi Mendel had told me during our meetings. "You are leaving this world a better place than it was when you found it, Abby."

And it was true. In the days and weeks following her death, her family was flooded with remembrances from not just her wide circle of friends, but from her elementary school teachers and other people she hadn't seen in twenty years. She had seemingly touched every person she had ever encountered.

After Abby died I wept. I cried over the loss of one of my deepest friendships, with a woman who had been able to see through the broken girl I was when we met, and the loss of a person who had taught me how to be a better person, a loving mother, and a true friend. I wept for her family most of all, for the exquisite pain and

## After This

unending questions they would all be left with in the wake of her loss.

---

Medium Fleur closes her eyes again, seeming to listen to someone or something that I can't hear.

"I've got a female here," she says. "Her death is quicker of nature, but there is definitely a lead-up to her passing. There's a real feeling of being in and out of the hospital and doctors just not knowing what to do.

"As she comes forward I see her traveling, always needing to explore the world. I see her hiking, see her in the outdoors, that this was very important to her."

Abby was definitely those things. She traveled the world in her career, working in places like Beijing, Austria, and South Korea. And she was always physically active, having worked as an aerobics instructor for a time in New York, and sharing a love of hiking and rock climbing with her husband.

I nod at her, waiting for more.

"She keeps saying 'best friend, best friend,' showing me an energy of you guys being very close. This is someone you've known for an extended period of time," Fleur says, and I feel flush with gratitude, still feeling undeserving for having had such a deep friendship with someone I admired so much.

"I know that she's also recognizing watching over little children in the world. She's watching over kids; this feels very important. She's saying, 'these kids, these kids, these kids,' showing me that she's beside them every step of the way."

I nod, tears brimming in my eyes now. Sharing motherhood with Abby was one of my favorite aspects of our friendship. Abby became a mother a few years before I did, and was always there for me when I had questions or trouble figuring out breast-feeding or sleep schedules. Her approach to motherhood was a calm and loving one, and I always admired how she spoke to her children, not just as the toddlers they were, but as though she could see the people they would become. It seems utterly unfair to me that they have been robbed of her presence.

"She talks about you having a connection to her family after her passing," Fleur continues, "and I do see you around her children. And she is wanting to just thank you for everything you've done in that regard. That feels really special for her. She wants to thank you for everything you've done to help them move forward."

Tears are dripping down my cheeks now. All of us who were friends with Abby have extended ourselves to her husband and children, and being one of the closest geographically, I have been spending time with them since she died.

In fact, two days before this appointment with Fleur I traveled to Boston for Abby's memorial service, something that her family had put off for a couple of months following her death, and I have just returned home last night. It was a hard weekend, a group of us, including Abby's husband and children, convening at the home of Abby's childhood friend Tarsha.

It was surreal to be with the same group of women who had gathered eight years ago as bridesmaids in Abby's wedding, together again to pay tribute to her too-short life, and to help support the small family she'd left behind.

Each night in Boston we worked as a group to get all the kids in the house to bed, trying to relieve her young husband of the overwhelming task of now caring for their two small children on his own. With my own daughters back home in Los Angeles, the night before the service I lay down with Abby's daughter, Julia, and Tarsha's son, Joseph, reading them stories and trying to lull them to sleep, while

## After This

the rest of the adults in the house worked to wrangle the other children to bed. Julia snuggled into me and I wrapped my arms around her, not being able to fathom how Abby was no longer here to do this herself.

The next morning I stood with tears in my eyes as three-year-old Julia squirmed and giggled in her underwear on the bed before me. I held up a tiny dress bright with yellow and pink flowers, trying to coax her to get dressed before the memorial service. Finally I sat down on the side of the bed next to one of Abby's friends, Julie.

"Julia, it's time to get dressed now," I said gently, trying to keep my voice from wavering. "Look," I said, holding up the dress. "This belonged to your mama. She wore this when she was little."

Julia just giggled and squirmed away from us some more.

"Julia," I said, tickling the bottom of her foot. "Do you know how much your mommy loved you? Oh, sweet girl, she loved you so, so much."

Julia smiled up at me, and then giggled some more, oblivious to the significance of this day.

I stole a glance at Abby's friend. She had tears in her eyes too. Like me, she was wearing a formal navy blue dress. Abby's husband was downstairs trying to get their seven-year-old son dressed; soon we would all leave for the church.

Finally, with a promise of cookies if she complied, I pulled the dress over Julia's head, and as I was fastening the buttons on the back, tears dripped freely down my cheeks, and I remembered how eight years ago I helped Abby get dressed for her wedding. I knew in that moment that had the situation been reversed, and I had died instead of Abby, she would have been the one right there with my girls, helping them get dressed for *my* memorial service, telling them how much I loved them.

I'm thinking about all this when Fleur begins speaking again.

"I also see here people speaking at a funeral, at a memorial, and that feels significant. She just wants to say thank you, thank you, thank you, from the bottom of her heart. As she connects with me about that she talks about rain being important for some reason, and rain being very significant, either on that day, or in connection to that. She just wants you to know that she was there," Fleur says.

The memorial was beautiful, a large handful of Abby's friends taking turns eulogizing her with meaningful stories and promises to continue to uphold the values and love Abby had embodied. It also rained that day, a steady drizzle all that morning and afternoon.

I'm crying even more now, thinking about Abby being there with all of us two days ago, but what Fleur says next is the thing that will stay with me for the rest of my life.

"I know you were there with her little girl. . . . I'm seeing the girl getting on a dress. I don't know if you helped her get on her dress, but she wants you to know she was with you at that time. It just feels to me very significant that what you said to her little girl recently has really helped your friend to know that she's in good hands. And I do feel that you'll continue to be a part of that family and continue to love them and aid them. I really feel like this woman comes in and recognizes you as a sister. She knows that you'll be there for her family as they continue forward."

I sit there across from Fleur in this bright office on a Monday morning in Los Angeles, just crying and nodding.

"You were one of her closest friends, one of her best friends," Fleur continues. "You had a very, very strong connection. You were there when she had her children and as she grew into motherhood, and that you were there to see all of it feels incredibly important to her. She says you obviously know what it's like to lose a mother at a young age, so you can be there for her little children because you'll be able to use that wisdom and that comfort and that light. She also recognizes that you were already writing a book before her passing but now she's unexpectedly included in it. And I do feel that you spoke about this before her passing and that it was kind of a joke of some sort, like, 'Well, now you're going to be in the book.' And I just feel that that is significant."

Here I start laughing through my tears. It's true. In those last days I had told Abby that I would include her in this book.

"I'm also wanting to talk about a letter that was written," Fleur says. "I don't know if she wrote letters to her kids, but this is very important. I feel like they're sealed up in envelopes to be given later. I know that she just wants to say that she really put her heart and soul into those letters."

In her last few weeks of life Abby did everything she could to leave messages for her children. She wrote a series of letters, one of which was sealed with the words "To be opened at any time" on it, and her husband told me about it on the day of the service.

"I just get this feeling that she really wants her children to have them," Fleur says. "She loves these children so, so much. And I feel like all these messages from her today are really in connection to them, in terms of making sure they're okay."

I nod at her, wiping at my tears.

"She also wants to thank you for the candles for some reason. There is recognition for the candles. I just see the lighting of multiple candles. She just wants to thank you for that."

I think about my silly little table at home, the one that I've been standing before for months now, lighting candles. I've lit them so many times for Abby, closing my eyes and telling her how much I love her, telling her that I'm trying to help with her children, that I hope she's okay wherever she is. My god, has she been watching me do this the whole time?

When I finally leave Fleur's office, I feel peaceful. Although

Abby's death has been a tragically sad one, I know that all of us who loved her have done everything we can to help take care of her family and give her children love and nurturing in her absence. After seeing Fleur I feel confident that Abby knows this, and that she can feel peaceful herself wherever she is. It's the only thing I would want if I were in her place.

When I get home I stand before my table one more time, and light my candles. My hands are shaking as I touch the match to the wicks. I watch the flames take hold and I close my eyes, letting myself feel all of them—Julie, my mother, my father, and Abby—standing around me as I do this.

They've always been with me. I know that now.

## After This

Dear Vera and Jules,

I've just come home from Boston, and Vera, you were so mad that I went away without you.

"Why didn't you take us with you?" you asked, not knowing that I had gone for my friend Abby's memorial service.

"Oh, because, sweetie, it was a hard weekend and I needed to be there to help with things. Do you remember my friend Abby?"

"Owen and Julia's mom?" you said.

"Yes, Owen and Julia's mommy," I replied.

Vera, you recounted a time two years ago when we had gone to the beach with all three of them. Owen had found a little crab in the sand, and as I held it out in my palm to show you, it sunk its little pincers into my finger. I yelped in surprise and flung it toward the ocean. Somehow the memory of this little moment was cemented in your mind, and every time I mention Abby you bring it up. You did again now and I smiled at the memory.

"Well, Owen and Julia's mom, Abby, died, and I went to Boston for the memorial service," I told you.

"She died?" you asked. "Owen and Julia don't have a mommy anymore?"

"Well," I replied carefully, "they will always have a mommy. Abby will always be their mommy."

"Will they get a new mommy now?" you asked.

"No, sweetie, it doesn't work that way," I told you.

"Abby was their one and only mommy, just as I am your one and only mommy."

"Oh," you said, looking down and picking at the cuff of your pants. You've decided just recently that you no longer want to wear dresses, only shorts and pants, because that's what five-year-old girls wear, and in that moment I could only think about how both grown-up and yet childlike you seemed.

"Can Owen and Julia still talk to Abby?" you asked then.

"Of course they can, sweetie. Just like how you and I talk to each other in our heads when I'm traveling or far away. They can talk to her like that and I think she can hear them."

You nodded. "And it's like the butterfly too, right? Owen and Julia can still love their mommy like we still love the butterfly?"

"Exactly," I said, and relief flooded through me when you said this.

All I want you girls to know about death is that it does not erase love. If that's the only thing I teach you before I go, I will be content.

Just promise me that you will always open yourselves up to the unknown, to the possibility of anything, to the idea that there are things happening all around us that we cannot see or imagine. Open yourself up to the idea that we are connected in ways that seem impossible. If you open yourself up to the idea that love never dies, then all you have to do is close your eyes and let yourself feel it.

You have done nothing for the past five years but grow and laugh and cry and paint messy things and spill

## After This

food and ride bikes and pick flowers and marvel at the world, and I could not be prouder of you. The two of you are my heart. You have completed me; you have made me who I am. You have made me remember that the world is full of magic, and that life and death are inherently beautiful endeavors.

You have made me realize that I am still connected to my own parents, that their love for me exists yet today, even though they are gone.

Thank you endlessly for coming into my life, for healing me, for making me whole, and for making me realize that love is all that matters.

I love you to the moon and back. I love you as big as the universe. I love you forever.

*Mama*

# Epilogue

The day I flew home from Abby's memorial service in Boston, my flight had been endlessly turbulent. My old flying fears resurfaced, after watching Abby's family struggle to go on without her and thinking about what my own daughters would face if I died young. As the plane rocked back and forth I gripped the armrest and squeezed my eyes shut, whispering a silent prayer in my head that I would make it home to my little girls that night.

But then suddenly I remembered what it had felt like helping Abby's daughter get dressed for the service the day before. I recalled the resolute knowledge that Abby would have done the same for me. I thought about how if I died, I would have friends just like she did, helping my daughters continue to feel my love surrounding them.

And then I remembered the night I went into labor with Vera, my first. I had been intent on having a natural childbirth, partially out of my apprehension surrounding Western medicine, and partly out of a desire to experience something that our bodies are naturally equipped to do. But as my labor deepened and the contractions grew stronger and stronger, I struggled to stay calm. The pain was immense and I suddenly doubted that I could withstand the experience.

In those panicked moments I remember drawing on the knowledge that a few of my friends, Abby in particular, had chosen this route when birthing their own children. And there in the birthing suite in that hospital in Chicago, I thought about her, about this friend of mine, this woman just like me with her own fears and insecurities and adventures, going through this exact experience. And when another contraction pulsed through my body I breathed through it, comforted by the knowledge that if Abby could do this, so could I.

And that's what I thought about on the plane, as I feared my own death, as I feared leaving my children behind when they are young. *Abby did this,* I thought to myself. *And if she could do it, I can too. And if I die right now on this airplane, I'll be with her, with my sweet friend on the other side, watching all those we left behind care for each other in our absence.* The plane finally leveled out and I took a deep breath, grateful not just that I would likely get home that night, but that everything would be okay if I didn't.

Even though I walked away from all my forays into the afterlife without any real answers to what actually happens when we die, I realized that it doesn't matter. All of the journeys I've embarked upon in my research have left me feeling like whatever it is will be okay, that all we can do here on earth is do the best we can until we get to the other side, whatever that looks like.

After my last visit to Abby, a few days before she died, I came home and sat on my little patio staring up at the bright blue California sky. A tiny plane arced through the clouds and I made myself answer a question someone had recently asked me when I told them about this book.

What do I most *want* to happen when we die?

It was a question I had never quite posed to myself. And the answer was one I couldn't stop thinking about as I watched my friend live out her last days.

An immediate sense of peace. Of calm and stillness. An instant knowing. An innate understanding of what this was all about. I am filled with understanding about my life. From the very moments of my birth to the final seconds of my death. All of it makes sense.

The images pass through me—my childhood and adolescence, my parents and their deaths. Every relationship, however deep or even fleeting, crystallizes in such a way that it seems utterly impossible for it to have happened any other way. Every mistake I ever made, every sorrow or heartache illuminated in a beauty that assures me that all of it was simply part of the fabric of the life I lived.

The peace and understanding of what it was all about is so great and so true that when I think of those I love whom I have left behind—my children and family, my friends and partners, even my pets—I do not wish them free of suffering. I do not wish them free of sadness or mourning, because I know that those things are part of the very essence of what it means to be human.

Here in this place I am part of a collective energy. I am the magic that makes trees grow and water flow. I am the liquid gold that lives within each cell of a human body. I am the breeze that pushes across the sand and the rain that falls in the forest. I am no longer Claire Bidwell Smith.

And that is okay.

What I am now is so simple and true. It is so different from the complex and painful and beautiful experience of being an individual human being. I see now how trapped we are in our human bodies, how all of our pain and suffering comes from our separateness.

For the truth is that we are not separate. We are all made up of the same essence. We come from the same source. We are each other. But in the human experience we are forced to feel contained within these limbs, these organs, these hearts and minds.

The pain of being human comes from feeling alone, from feeling separate. The pain comes from our constant need to connect, to love, to attempt to form unions with those we encounter, with those we love. The pain comes because we cannot do that within the restrictions of these bodies.

But this is also where the beauty is. The horrific and complex beauty of being a human. Of feeling alone, of having one lifetime, or many over and over, in which we strive to encase ourselves within this singular experience. The pain comes from this not being the truth of what we are.

We are all the same. We are all connected. We are each other.

This life. These bodies. It is an illusion that we cannot see or understand, but that teaches us what love is. It hurts when we lose people, because we think the love is gone. But the truth is that we are the love. We are those people whom we have lost. They are us.

And here in this place that we return to, this place where we flow again with each other, when we are all of each other all over again, where there is no separateness, we understand why we had to feel that way. We feel immense gratitude for the experience of pain and suffering and loss. We understand that we come back here in order to immerse ourselves in the magic that makes plants burst forth from the earth. We come back here to make that magic even stronger, to evolve it so that the universe may evolve as well.

And we know that for all whom we have left behind, whatever comes of their lives here on earth is exactly what they must experience in order to continue the wonder of it all.

And for as much as we feel peaceful and beautiful here in this

## After This

place, we yearn to return to all the wondrous suffering and pain and harsh glory of being human.

And so we do.

We know that each time we return it will be to learn another lesson. To create a broader understanding. To make this world a more beautiful place, no matter how much it hurts to do so.

In this place we know that all the fear and anxiety and pain we experience in our lives on earth is really something quite magnificent. That only in this way, only in this separateness, can we learn what it means to be whole.

I am able to see my daughters moving through their lives. They are making mistakes. They are falling in love. They are creating art and structure. They are shifting through a thousand identities. They are crossing through all the places in the world, searching for the answers that drive us all to get up each morning.

I see them weeping and I see them laughing. I see them teetering on the edge of confusion and pain, and a thousand different choices. I see them in all their perfection. I see that every moment of who they are in this brief lifetime is perfect.

And I know that they will be okay, that everything they experience is perfect.

I do not mourn them. I do not fear for them. I do not miss them. I am them. And they are me.

All of us, we are each other. There is no such thing as good-bye.

# ACKNOWLEDGMENTS

This book was born out of the deep love I have for the people in my life, and with that, I must acknowledge them.

First to my brilliant and luminous editor, Denise Roy. You have championed this book since our very first conversation, and without your guidance and emotional wisdom I never could have seen it through. Not to mention that there is no one else I could imagine charging crystals with.

To Wendy Sherman, who is both a surrogate mother and the best literary agent a writer could ask for. Your ability to always take my calls and talk me off ledges I didn't even realize I was on has been the saving grace of my last four years. I don't know what I would do without you.

To all my crazy writer friends who supported me emotionally through this process— Sarah Jio, Jillian Lauren, Mark Sarvas, Will Richter, Aidan Donnelley Rowley, Jenny Feldon, Kelle Hampton, Meredith Maran, Dani Shapiro, and Jane Green— I am unbearably

## Acknowledgments

grateful for all the thousand conversations I had with each of you about why we write. Thank you for your wisdom and friendship.

Thank you to Kyra Paliobagis and Kelly Bergin for taking such good care of the girls while I worked on this book. During the height of trying to meet my deadline, when Vera told me that she felt like she didn't have a mother anymore, I still knew that my girls would emerge unscathed because they were in such good hands.

Writing this book was nothing short of a spiritual experience and I couldn't have done it without the support of so many people I am lucky to call my friends. Elizabeth Fox, Mick Kubiak, Jennifer Beck Furber, Christa Parravani, Lien Ta, Elizabeth Garrett, Francesca McCaffery, Holly Bond, Joan Lynch, Melissa Pope, Lisa Whelan, Jennifer Mack, and Tarsha Benevento. Thank you for endless conversations about life, death, motherhood, astrology, past lives, and séances.

Cat Kabira, sitting next to you on that flight to Boston all those years ago was fated by the highest order. If there is anyone I have known for a thousand lifetimes it is you. Your generous heart and open mind are true gifts to the world.

Gratitude to Rabbi Mendel Simons and Dr. BJ Miller for such fantastic conversations about life, death, and the beyond. Our talks illuminated my journey with a light that continues to shine in my life.

Thank you to all of my clients, past and present, whose lives and stories have inspired me to no end. I hold each of you in a special place in my heart, and our time together has changed me in the most profound ways possible. Thank you to Thea Harvey for helping make my vision of grief retreats a reality. And deep thanks to Lesli A. Johnson for being a mentor and guide to me in this profession—your wisdom and compassion are inspiring.

Finally, to Greg Boose, who is the best father Veronica and

## Acknowledgments

Juliette could ever ask for. The love and understanding you give to our daughters is something that will see them through their lives and make them into the incredible women they are sure to become.

Veronica and Juliette, you are my heart. One day when you're older you will read this book and shake your heads over how crazy your mother was, or still is. Thank you for showing me the true depths of my heart and for teaching me that love never, ever dies.

# SOURCES

**Preface**

Insect Lore Live Butterfly Garden
http://www.insectlore.com

Kübler-Ross, Elisabeth. *On Life After Death*. Celestial Arts, 2008.

**Chapter One**

Advocate Hospice, Chicago
http://www.advocatehealth.com/Hospice

John Edward
Edward, John. *After Life*. Sterling Ethos, 2010.
Edward, John. *One Last Time*. Berkley Trade, 1999.
http://johnedward.net

**Chapter Two**

Delphina, medium
http://www.spiritguiding.com

**Chapter Three**

826LA, Nonprofit Tutoring Center
http://826la.org

# Sources

Todd Burpo, author and speaker
Burpo, Todd. *Heaven Is for Real*. Thomas Nelson, 2010.
http://heavenisforreal.net

C3 San Diego Church
http://c3sandiego.com

Rabbi Mendel, Young Jewish Professionals
http://www.yjplosangeles.com

Bill Wiese, author and speaker
Wiese, Bill. *23 Minutes in Hell*. Charisma House, 2006.
https://www.soulchoiceministries.com

## Chapter Four

Michael C. Brown, past-life regression
http://www.dejaviewpastlives.com

Gahl Sasson, past-life regression and astrology
Sasson, Gahl. *Cosmic Navigator: Design Your Destiny with Astrology and Kabbalah*. Weisner Books, 2008.
http://cosmicnavigator.com

Brian Weiss, past-life regression
Weiss, Brian. *Many Lives, Many Masters*. Fireside, 1988.
http://www.brianweiss.com

## Chapter Five

Eben Alexander, author and speaker
Alexander, Eben. *Proof of Heaven: A Neurosurgeon's Journey into the Afterlife*. Simon and Schuster, 2012.
http://www.ebenalexander.com

Julie Beischel, author and scientist
Beischel, Julie. *Among Mediums: A Scientist's Quest for Answers*. Windbridge Institute LLC, 2013.

## Sources

Beischel, Julie. *Meaningful Messages: Making the Most of Your Mediumship Reading.* Windbridge Institute LLC, 2013.
http://www.windbridge.org/index.htm

Theresa Caputo, medium
Caputo, Theresa. *You Can't Make This Stuff Up: Life-Changing Lessons from Heaven.* Atria Books, 2014.
http://www.theresacaputo.com

Forever Family Foundation, Afterlife Conferences
https://www.foreverfamilyfoundation.org

James Van Praagh, medium
Van Praagh, James. *Talking to Heaven: A Medium's Message of Life After Death.* Signet, 1999.
http://www.vanpraagh.com

### Chapter Six

Jon Kabat-Zinn, author
Kabat-Zinn, Jon. *Wherever You Go, There You Are: Mindfulness Meditation in Everyday Life.* Hyperion, 2005.

Thich Nhat Hanh
Nhat Hanh, Thich. *The Miracle of Mindfulness: An Introduction to the Practice of Meditation.* Beacon Press, 1999.

Frank Ostaseski
*Being a Compassionate Companion* (audio CD). Zen Hospice Project, 2003.
http://www.mettainstitute.org

Zen Hospice Project
http://www.zenhospice.org

### Chapter Seven

Edelman, Hope. *Motherless Daughters.* Da Capo Lifelong Books, 2014.
http://www.hopeedelman.com

# Sources

Amanda Foulger, shaman
http://www.amandafoulger.com/about2.html

The Foundation for Shamanic Studies
http://www.shamanism.org

Michael Harner, author and founder of the Foundation for Shamanic Studies
Harner, Michael. *The Way of the Shaman*. HarperOne, 1990.

## Chapter Eight

Cat Kabira, yoga instructor and craniosacral therapist
http://www.catkabira.com

Kaelin, Angela. *How to Communicate with Spirits: Seances, Ouija Boards and Summoning*. Winter Tempest Books, 2013.

Ouija Board
http://winning-moves.com/product/ouija.asp

## Chapter Nine

Paula Shaw, medium and intuitive
http://www.soulfulguiding.com

Shriver, Maria. *What's Heaven?* Golden Books Adult Publishing, 2007.

## Chapter Ten

Fleur, psychic medium
http://mediumfleur.com

Made in the USA
Las Vegas, NV
01 December 2024